CAN AMERICA SURVIVE?

ALSO BY BEN STEIN

HOW TO RUIN YOUR LIFE
(also available as an audio book)

HOW TO RUIN YOUR LOVE LIFE

HOW TO RUIN YOUR FINANCIAL LIFE

HOW TO RUIN . . . Book Collection
(comprises the three titles above)

★★★

ALSO BY BEN STEIN AND PHIL DEMUTH

YES, YOU CAN BE A SUCCESSFUL INCOME INVESTOR!:
Reaching for Yield in Today's Market
(available March 2005)

YES, YOU CAN STILL RETIRE IN COMFORT!:
The Baby-Boom Retirement Crisis and How to Beat It
(available September 2005)

★★★

All of the above are available at your local bookstore,
or may be ordered by visiting the distributors for
New Beginnings Press:

Hay House USA: **www.hayhouse.com**
Hay House Australia: **www.hayhouse.com.au**
Hay House UK: **www.hayhouse.co.uk**
Hay House South Africa: **orders@psdprom.co.za**

★★★

CAN AMERICA SURVIVE?

The Rage of the Left,
the Truth, and What to Do about It

Ben Stein and Phil DeMuth

NBP

NEW BEGINNINGS PRESS

an imprint of
HAY HOUSE, INC.
Carlsbad, California
London • Sydney • Johannesburg
Vancouver • Hong Kong

Published by: New Beginnings Press, Carlsbad, California

Distributed in the United States of America by: Hay House, Inc., P.O. Box 5100, Carlsbad, CA 92018-5100 • *Phone:* (760) 431-7695 or (800) 654-5126 • *Fax:* (760) 431-6948 or (800) 650-5115 • www.hayhouse.com • *Distributed in Australia by:* Hay House Australia Pty. Ltd., 18/36 Ralph St., Alexandria NSW 2015 • *Phone:* 612-9669-4299 • *Fax:* 612-9669-4144 • www.hayhouse.com.au • *Distributed in the United Kingdom by:* Hay House UK, Ltd. • Unit 62, Canalot Studios • 222 Kensal Rd., London W10 5BN • *Phone:* 44-20-8962-1230 • *Fax:* 44-20-8962-1239 • www.hayhouse.co.uk • *Distributed in the Republic of South Africa by:* Hay House SA (Pty), Ltd., P.O. Box 990, Witkoppen 2068 • *Phone/Fax:* 2711-7012233 • orders@psdprom.co.za • *Distributed in Canada by:* Raincoast • 9050 Shaughnessy St., Vancouver, B.C. V6P 6E5 • *Phone:* (604) 323-7100 • *Fax:* (604) 323-2600

Library of Congress Cataloging-in-Publication Data

Stein, Benjamin, 1944-
  Can America survive? : the rage of the left, the truth, and what to do about it / Ben Stein & Phil DeMuth.
     p. cm.
  Includes bibliographical references.
  ISBN 1-4019-0333-9 (hardcover)
  1. Liberalism—United States. 2. Conservatism—United States. 3. United States—Politics and government—2001- I. DeMuth, Phil, 1950- II. Title.
  JC574.2.U6S73 2004
  320.51'3'0973—dc22
                              2004005821

ISBN 1-4019-0333-9

07 06 05 04   4 3 2 1
1st printing, July 2004

Printed in United States of America

For Tommy, Rani, and Olivia

CONTENTS

ACKNOWLEDGMENTS
by Ben Stein

"A nation is marked by the men and women it chooses to honor." Thus said John F. Kennedy, a liberal Democrat who loved his country. So it goes with individual citizens.

The roll call of the people I choose to honor and who inspired me starts with Col. Dale Denman, Jr., my father-in-law. He came from the small town of Prescott, Arkansas, to go to West Point just as World War II was getting under way. He graduated from the Point in 1944 and went to Europe to fight the Nazis. He battled across France, Germany, and Austria; went hand-to-hand against the SS; and ran through Nazi machine-gun and sniper fire to get to a farmhouse to call in artillery fire on German positions that were pinning down his unit. For this, unsolicited, he won the Silver Star.

Twenty years later, in middle age, he fought in the jungle trails of Vietnam. On his 43rd birthday, he was in a rice paddy in black pajamas pretending to be Vietnamese, setting up an ambush while he was halfway submerged. In the ensuing firefight, Col. Denman's leadership kept his charges of the South Vietnamese Army from being massacred. For this he won a second Silver Star, also unsolicited.

In the 20 years in between World War II and Vietnam, my father-in-law served all over the world in dusty posts, often far from home, and often in cold isolation. His brave wife, Norma Jean (now deceased), had to travel around the world, making a home and taking care of her two daughters, Dale and Alex (who became my wife). Norma Jean, Alex, and Dale also served their country; even though the sacrifices of military families are rarely mentioned, they're no less real. These families also deserve to be honored, and they're very much in my memory and thoughts day by day.

My wife's uncle, Bob Denman, was an Army lieutenant in some of the darkest days, months, and years of Korea. In one particularly harrowing engagement, his unit was pinned down by a North Korean machine gunner—Bob went around behind that man with a carbine and shot him, which saved his platoon. His major recommended that Bob get the Silver Star. "No," said the young lieutenant, "I only want it if everyone in my unit gets one." But his major told him that it wasn't a unit citation. So Bob declined to authorize receiving the medal, stating, "I only did what everyone else in my unit did."

After the war, he quietly went back to Arkansas and lived as an executive of an industrial fan company. I had to pry this story out of him with pliers—he never talks about it and never brags, and neither does his brother. They inspire me and move me to tears. World War II could never have been won without men like this, and neither could the Cold War have been waged.

My grandfather, David Stein, came to this country as a small child from Russia without a father. He joined the U.S. Cavalry at age 16 with papers he borrowed from his older brother. He served all over the Western U.S. and then fought in the Philippines against the Aguinaldo insurrection. (My nephew, Jonathan, who, like me, is a history buff, has his great-grandfather's sharpshooter's medal.) He was a skilled tool-and-die maker at Ford during and after the First World War, then became unemployed through most of the Great Depression—yet he never flagged in his love of country. My grandmother on my father's side felt the same way, as did my mother's parents (all Republicans, but this is totally incidental).

My father, Herbert Stein, was a relentless patriot. He devoted his life largely to public service, starting before the Second World War, during which he served in the Navy. He often taught me that once a human being was born an American, he was blessed beyond what the ordinary mortal could imagine. He grew up facing significant anti-Semitic prejudice—yet he was able to put it into a noble context and realize that as annoying as discrimination in this nation often was, it was zero compared with what Jews had to face in all other countries and in all other eras. I can well recall that at the one and only Stein family reunion in the mid-1990s, my father gave a speech in which he said that he was grateful to his ancestors for all they did—but above all, for coming to America.

My mother was also a fierce patriot and an unbending anti-Communist. She'd gone to Barnard College, a part of Columbia University, in the early- and mid-1930s, when Communists were everywhere and seemed to be the leading ideological edge of the intellectual class. My mother was never taken in and spent most of her life fighting and arguing against the collectivists wherever and whenever the occasion presented itself. She also preached to me endlessly that America was the greatest thing that had ever happened to mankind and that we should consider ourselves blessed beyond measure by reason of living in the USA.

From all of these relatives I have taken inspiration, and I owe them all deeply.

I had great teachers in the public schools of Montgomery County, Maryland, in the 1950s and 1960s. To these fine men and women, it came naturally to praise America and to teach their students that love of their country was an integral part of mental health. In those long-forgotten days, teachers believed it was their job to build moral character and that patriotism was a major part of that character—and I'm grateful for it. I don't have anywhere near the strength of character of many people around me, but what little I do have is owed largely to my teachers.

The parents of my childhood best friend, David Lee Scull, were also exemplars of patriotism. David's father, also named David, had been a World War II hero and was a local political leader and a man of extreme inspiration. His wife, son, and daughter were all the same kind of people, and their love of country and devotion to doing what's right (even if it's unpopular) has moved me since 1953.

I had some superb teachers in college as well, especially Mr. Rothstein, an expert on the history of Eastern Europe since World War II. That history told much about what Communism does to a nation and a people, and it terrified me. (I don't know his first name because in those days at Columbia, students only called their teachers "Mister.")

In law school, I was taught by superb exemplars of love of country and liberty, especially Larry Simon, Robert Bork, and Alex Bickel. (I never actually had Alex Bickel as a teacher, but his spirit of fair play and reverence for the Constitution pervaded the very halls of the Sterling Law Building at Yale.)

After law school, my main inspiration was Richard Nixon. Nixon, crucified for offending the liberal establishment with nails he handed them himself, stood up to the ultra-Left jackal pack his whole life. Despite their nonstop attacks on him, he ended the war in Vietnam; brought back the POWs; started nuclear-missile reduction talks with Russia and signed the first arms-reduction treaty; and opened relations with China so that Russia would never be able to win the Cold War, thereby setting the stage for the end of the Cold War. Nixon also ended the 1973 Arab-Israeli War by standing up for Israel despite a lifetime of having been tormented by left-wing Jewish Americans. This was a stand for principle such as I haven't seen from any Democratic President in my lifetime. (The mystery of why American

Jews prefer Democrat Presidents who thumb their noses at Israel never fails to stupefy me.) I wish all young Americans would know Nixon as the man I knew him to be—above all, he was a peacemaker, and I'll never turn my back on him.

When I had the privilege of working for Richard Nixon, I also had the extreme pleasure of working with two inspiring men in offices right next to me: John R. Coyne, Jr., and Aram Bakshian. These two men, both far more capable and seasoned speech writers than I was, were historians as well as scribes, and they've been instructors and catechizers ever since we began our work together in November of 1973. (Can it really be so long ago?) I was also privileged to work with or near Ray Price; Pat Buchanan; William Safire (who left just as I was coming on board); Ken Khachigian; and our boss, Dave Gergen. They were and are all impressive men from whom I learned a great deal. There's much that Pat Buchanan writes with which I disagree, but his heart is in the right place on America, and he's a longtime friend.

When Mr. Nixon was forced to leave office prematurely in an unearned disgrace, I was lucky enough to work for several months for Gerald R. Ford (a fellow graduate of Yale Law School), who was an immensely kind and decent man.

Besides my father, my main source of knowledge at the White House was the dapper, brilliant, and well-tested Peter M. Flanigan. This investment banker/statesman belongs to a more genteel age; and his devotion to me when I was at the White House and afterward when we were both on Wall Street (although at very different levels), touches me endlessly.

When I left the White House, I was lucky enough to work for Bob Bartley at *The Wall Street Journal*. Bob is a major icon in the pantheon of defenders of liberty, and his fearless defense of freedom and law amazed and encouraged me every day. Long after I left the *Journal*, I came to sharp disagreements with him as to various issues of finance and shareholders' litigation, but I never lost my reverence for the man, and feel it keenly still. He died far, far too early and belongs to a select group who may be called genuinely irreplaceable.

It's been my great pleasure to write for *The American Spectator* for more than 30 years. This small but brave magazine has stood against the current of liberal and anti-American conformism in the world of letters. Wlady Pleszcynzski, managing editor, and Bob Tyrrell, editor in chief, took on Bill Clinton and exposed a wealth of interesting facts about him—and they never backed down in the face of any threats. Both men are still close friends, and I hope to write for them for the rest of my life.

For about ten years, I wrote a column for the late, much-lamented *Los Angeles Herald-Examiner.* My first editor there, Jim Bellows, Navy flyer, editor, and innovator extraordinaire, has supported and encouraged me for two and a half decades. I've also been writing for *Barron's* for about 18 years now. Their top dogs, Alan Abelson and Jim Meagher, were and are fighting editors and writers who put me on the map as a breaker of financial fraud. From them, as from so many others mentioned here, I learned not to back down.

I was inspired by Ann Coulter and Dinesh D'Souza; as well as by my co-author's brother, Chris DeMuth, the wildly successful head of the indispensable foundation of American liberties and citadel of freedom, The American Enterprise Institute. Oddly enough, I was also moved to write this little book by my friend and frequent adversary, Al Franken. I thought that if he could write a book about his beliefs, so could I, and I did.

In the specific writing of this book, I was aided beyond measure by my co-author, Phil DeMuth, who really did much more than half of the work. My wife also helped me with ideas and suggestions, as did my sister, Rachel Epstein; her husband,

Melvin; and my niece and nephew (both historians), Jonathan Epstein and Emily Landau. I thank again my agent, the smokin' Lois Wallace, and I especially thank everyone at New Beginnings Press, particularly the most easy-to-work-with editors on earth.

But above all, my part of this book is an homage to my mother and father. In many ways, it's no more than a lengthy restatement of the homilies by which they lived their lives and loved this country. For the many errors and omissions that are undoubtedly in here, as well as for the mistakes of interpretation and understanding which are also inevitable, I am solely responsible.

★★★ ★★★

ACKNOWLEDGMENTS
by Phil DeMuth

L ooking through a box of old photographs, I come upon
an uncle I never met. His name was Tommy Schaiell, and
he's wearing a sailor's uniform and smiling from the stoop
outside a duplex on Byron Street in Chicago. The date on the
photograph is May 1942, and he's 20 years old. The photo is
signed, "Love and kisses, Tommy."

I recalled that Tommy, my mom's kid brother, died in the
Navy in World War II, but I'd never really inquired past this point.
He was just some dead relative I'd never met, of little relevance
to my life. Now my parents are themselves gone, and there's no
one left to ask about him.

I Googled the name of his ship, the USS *Enterprise,* and after
wading through several hundred *Star Trek* tribute pages, I found
the ship's muster of all the names of the thousands of men who
served on her, including, it turns out, one Thomas W. Schaiell,
GM 2/c, KIA. GM 2/c turns out to be shorthand for gunner's
mate, second class. He would have been assigned to fire the ship's
guns and handle ammunition, and would have been paid $114
a month. I already knew that KIA meant "killed in action."

I discover that Tommy died on Monday, August 24, 1942,
during the Battle of the Eastern Solomons. Admiral Yamamoto
launched Operation KA to crush the American carriers protecting Guadalcanal. At 4:55 P.M., two formations of Val dive-
bombers attacked the *Enterprise* group. The Japanese lost 29
planes in the aerial battle, but 30 survived to close in on the
ship. They lined up and pitched their dives, one plane every

seven seconds. The *Enterprise's* guns shelled 15 more of them out of the sky, but it wasn't enough.

At 5:14 P.M., a bomb pierced the wooden deck and exploded five levels below, rupturing the hull and causing the boat to list; 30 seconds later, a second bomb struck. Detonating on impact, it obliterated the aft starboard gun gallery and its crew, and the violence of the explosion was magnified by the ignition of the powder bags in the gun tub. Thirty-eight men died in that moment. A remarkable photograph on the Internet actually shows the gun gallery in flames, where Gunner's Mate Second Class Thomas W. Schaiell had been killed only moments earlier.

The U.S. won a victory that day, but I lost my Uncle Tommy. He never lived to see the postwar boom or Sputnik, and he never learned to do the Twist. He wasn't around the day JFK was shot, and he missed Woodstock and Watergate. No avuncular advice was dispensed at the personal landmarks of this nephew's life. He wasn't there at my college graduation or to dance at my wedding or at a wedding of his own. Instead, he gave his life for his country. I never knew I missed him until I found his photograph.

My father, Harry DeMuth, left his wife and baby daughter behind to serve in World War II as well. He rarely mentioned it, and I was too stupid to ask him very much about it while he was alive (please don't make this mistake with your father), but I've read up on it a little since. A major in the Army Air Force stationed in India, Dad "flew the hump," a euphemism for the transport of supplies across the Himalayan mountains over what came to be known as the "aluminum trail," strewn as it was with the wreckage of C-46s along the way. The planes took off regardless of weather, and often with only a rough guess as to the weight of the cargo and their ability to climb the mountain range while carrying it. This unglamorous job, in a backwater of World War II, actually proved more dangerous than flying combat missions. With the icy mountain peaks, the Japanese, and even the cannibals (!) in the jungles of Burma below, the odds of survival if your plane crashed weren't good. Yet my dad and millions just like him took the risk and ended up saving the world. I sometimes feel as if the memory of their service and sacrifice has been erased from my generation's Etch A Sketch, so this book is a very small flag planted in their honor.

My ancestors came to America with John Wesley and General Oglethorpe in 1736. It's said that when a great storm arose at sea during the crossing, the Moravians responded by singing hymns. The obstacles encountered by America's early settlers were formidable, yet they faced them with an immense faith. I sometimes feel as if we're living off the spiritual capital generated by our nation's founders, and we're running on fumes. That is another motive behind this book.

In my own little life, as far as acknowledgments go, I must mention Julia, *sine qua nihil* ("without whom I am nothing"), as well as the endless support of my family and friends. More immediately, our crackerjack researcher, Todd Weiner, of the American Enterprise Institute, has been extremely helpful. Any errors that have snuck into this book are all his fault (just kidding, Todd!). The editorial department at New Beginnings Press is a dream to work with, and forever spoiled is the writer who finds himself in its care. Finally, my co-author is a continuing source of instruction and inspiration. Take it from me: You learn more over lunch with Ben Stein than you will in most four-year colleges these days.

★★★ ★★★

INTRODUCTION

To get an idea of where this book is coming from, imagine the following scenario:

It's June 1942—six months after the land and naval forces of the United States were cruelly, brutally, and "suddenly and deliberately attacked" (in Roosevelt's immortal words) at Pearl Harbor, killing more than 2,500 men and women and sinking a large part of America's Pacific fleet. The people who did the bombing, the Japanese, have since attacked U.S. forces in the Philippines, routing our Marines, Navy, and Army there and capturing tens of thousands of prisoners. Those prisoners have then been mistreated in a ghastly manner involving brutal torture and murder. There have also been attacks on the U.S. forces at Wake Island and at other small outposts in the Pacific.

In Europe, Japan's principal ally, Nazi Germany, has declared war on the United States. German submarines are sinking American tankers and freighters at a breathtaking clip up and down the Atlantic seaboard and in the Gulf of Mexico; they've also defeated the French forces and have occupied a part of France. In addition, the Germans have attacked Russia after having subdued Poland, Czechoslovakia, Greece, the Baltic States, Norway, Belgium, Holland, Yugoslavia, and Albania. Throughout all of this, America's Democratic President is attempting to rally the nation and fight back against the aggressors.

Now imagine that on college campuses, the main focal point of student rallies is whether or not the United States is acting in a racist manner by fighting back against the Japanese in the Pacific. At demonstrations all across the country, young (and not-so-young) people scream bitter invective at Roosevelt for going to war against a people whose skin is a different color from our own. There are calls for his replacement and "a regime change" in Washington because FDR has fought a war against a different culture in an obvious effort to steal their resources.

In newspaper columns and at opposition meetings, FDR is called "a piece of s—t" and a "miserable failure" because he pro- voked the war by embargoing scrap-iron and oil exports to Japan. Masses gather on Washington streets to demand a new President who will negotiate with the Japanese, find an end to the war, and bring Americans home from overseas, where they might be in harm's way.

Mere mention of the ethnicity of the Japanese—who bombed Pearl Harbor and who are raging through China using that coun- try's POWs as bayonet dummies—is derided as race baiting and discrimination. Consciousness-raising sessions are held to explore the sensitivities of the Japanese and the Germans—to examine what in the American way of life might have been hurtful to those people, forcing them to turn to Nazism and Imperialism and to fire upon the Americans who have "shamed" them.

Every day newspapers bring a flood of articles about the Ameri- cans killed that day in the fighting, and a mass of hand-wringing about whether or not the men and women who died did so just to promote a hidden agenda of Roosevelt's.

Laws against sabotage and allowing surveillance of those sus- pected of espionage for Japan and Germany are the object of name- calling and bitterness at college rallies; and they're derided as unnecessary and harmful to the civil liberties that the nation is built upon. Powerful Republican figures in Congress wail about the anti-subversion and anti-sabotage acts, calling them subterfuges to allow FDR to create a dictatorial atmosphere in the United States and secure his power indefinitely.

Every attempt by Roosevelt to increase defense spending is met by a cry from the opposition, which claims that the money is wasted and would be better spent on more kindergartens and better pay for teachers. There is an attempt to build a large oil pipeline and highway up into Alaska to transfer oil and war material to a convenient shipping point; but environmentalists say that protecting the tundra is far more important to the future of America than prosecuting a racist war. The intense hue and cry against the efforts in Alaska reach such a crescendo that eventually a filibuster against the appropriation is mounted and the project is shelved. In the meantime, the Japanese seize several of the islands in the Bering Sea, which require the sacrifice of thousands of U.S. lives to dislodge them.

Meanwhile, the moral character of the President and his top aides is constantly challenged, and a nationwide lament is heard from the GOP that we need a man like Coolidge back in office, who would never have embarked on "foreign adventures" no matter what the provocation, but would have kept his nation focused on the problems at home. On talk shows and in newspaper columns, a constant barrage of belittlement is thrown at FDR, as he is blamed for failing to anticipate the attacks at Pearl Harbor.

A whispering campaign is even begun against him by Republicans competing for office—they allege that the President knew about the pending attacks but did nothing to stop them because he wanted to enmesh the U.S. in an imperialistic war to enrich munitions makers, British plutocrats, and Jewish financiers. A more public campaign holds that FDR has been waging the war incompetently— any number of GOP stalwarts could wage it faster, find the specific Japanese perpetrators who attacked Pearl Harbor (without demonizing a whole nation just because their traditions are different from ours), and end it without interfering with vital programs such as dismantling Roosevelt's New Deal.

There are some Republicans who endorse the war against Japan as long as it's waged in accordance with strict internationally created rules, but the overwhelming mass of GOP activists absolutely refuses to endorse fighting against Germany and Italy. This is a part of the war, they say, that doesn't need to be waged, since we know it was the Japanese who bombed Pearl Harbor, not the Germans or the Italians. (Plus, they reiterate that we shouldn't be in a war against all of Japan, but only have the police and FBI search out the specific Japanese who planned and executed the attack.)

The clear fact that the Germans and Italians endorsed the surprise raid on Pearl Harbor and are aiding the Japanese morally and materially is not, these people say, enough reason to create an entirely new front, at great cost in life and money. These GOP bigwigs demand that the U.S. stay well away from the European conflict until it's been proven that at least some of the pilots who bombed Pearl Harbor were actually Germans or Italians. They threaten to hold up spending for the war in the Pacific unless Roosevelt renounces any alliance with Britain and Russia against Germany and Italy.

Had this horrifying, bizarre alternative history actually taken place—that is, if our nation had been bitterly divided about whether to pursue World War II—it's questionable whether we could have beaten a determined and resourceful Axis. Regardless, winning the war would have been a far more protracted struggle, and the United States would have forfeited the moral high ground in Europe for half a century. England, our best friend, would have nearly bled to death. And the scenario mentioned above might well have meant the end of enlightened civilization for an unimaginably long period, as the Nazis and the Japanese would have dominated the world. Resistance at home to fighting World War II, along with a German victory, could very well have led to (in Winston Churchill's chilling words)

". . . a new Dark Ages, made more protracted by the lights of a perverted science."

Yet something very like this alternative history *is* happening in the United States and in many Western countries (especially the United Kingdom) right now.

The Enemy Within

A scant amount of time after the most destructive day in United States history since the Civil War—September 11, 2001—the fury of much of the opinionated classes in the United States has been directed against . . . the United States and its leadership. Instead of massive rallies showing rage against the Islamic terrorists who attacked America (and who are still attacking Americans), we have major rallies assailing the President for leading the war against terrorism.

Amazingly, in a nation where we've suffered so cruelly because of the insane jealousy of certain deranged souls in the Muslim world, there hasn't been one major demonstration against Islam or Islamists. This is in itself a stupefying testament to the magnanimity of the American spirit. But in what can hardly be called *sensible* or even *rational*, we've endured anguished questioning of ourselves over whether or not we're being fair to Muslims and Arabs by subjecting them to excessive scrutiny "merely" because the terrorists who continually attack the United States are Muslims and Arabs. The slightest sign of close inspection of air travelers because they're Arabs evokes near hysteria in the media and on college campuses.

What's far worse, though, is that instead of a logical and sound national mood of justice and retribution toward the people who attacked this nation, we have in many quarters a compulsion to aid the attackers by joining in! There's a "piling on" of verbal and moral assaults against the United States, often by United States citizens.

We had a foreign enemy, Saddam Hussein, who called us an "imperialistic, overreaching, and anti-human" power, one led by a "viper's son" named George W. Bush. Many leaders of the Democratic party, the "loyal opposition," as one might call it, didn't reply to this defamation with a united chorus of contempt—instead, they joined in. Over and over in the summer, fall, and winter of 2003, eight of the nine Democratic candidates for President spoke out not against terrorism, but against America and her leadership. According to those folks who wanted to be President—senators, former governors, U.S. representatives, and a minister of the Gospel—and their pals on the Democratic side of the aisle in Congress, America was a cowboy nation led by a corrupt buckaroo. These people told us that the whole war on terrorism as waged by George W. Bush (with the endorsement of the United States Congress, we might add) was a phony, "created in Texas" as Senator Edward Kennedy of Massachusetts said, made up only to solidify Bush's control of America. The one major exception to this party line has been Senator Joe Lieberman, the courageous and principled Democrat of Connecticut, who was knocked out of the running for the nomination early.

Measures to fight domestic terrorism as codified in the Patriot Act are derided by most of the leading Democrats as efforts to create a dictatorship and deprive Americans of their liberties under the Constitution. To hosannas of applause from college students, speakers allege that the real purpose of the war on terror is to allow Bush and Attorney General John Ashcroft to find out what books Americans are buying and taking from their libraries. Increased security is supposedly in the service of an effort to impose a right-wing dictatorship on America, and then on the world. (This commentary occurs despite the fact that as of this writing, in the late spring of 2004, not one person's library records or book-buying habits have been examined under the Patriot Act.)

If the mullahs had been writing the script themselves, they could hardly have done better.

America, the Land of Racism

Muslim extremists and other enemies of the U.S. allege that the American empire is really trying to impose the dominion of white, colonialist crusaders over nonwhite Muslim peoples. Boiled down to its essentials, the charge from these radicals is that American imperialistic power is itself powered by a wicked form of racism.

The Left in America shouts, "Right on!" Speakers from the topmost ranks of the Democratic party, led by Al Gore, former senator and longtime vice president under Bill Clinton, tell African Americans that they're being oppressed by a sort of racism that's so insidious and pervasive that it cannot be seen. Naturally it's wielded by Mr. Bush and his ilk, and is the ruling force in the lives of black men and women, according to far too many Democrat leaders.

The only cure for such racial prejudice is a "regime change" (the phrase comes from Senator John Kerry of Massachusetts, very possibly our next President) in Washington, or replacing the people who are fighting the war on terror with men and women who see battling domestic racism as a higher priority.

Do we really have imperialistic racism in the United States today? The fact is, we currently live in a society that, after an inexcusable period of horrible, ingrained, institutionalized bigotry, has become the most open and racially diverse industrial democracy in history. We have an America that's led by a black secretary of state, a black national security adviser, and a black secretary of education; and black men and women have reached the highest tiers of congressional and judicial power. Black men head two of the largest financial corporations in America (Merrill Lynch and American Express). Black men and women dominate the TV, music, and movie scenes and are towering figures in sports, commanding wages unimaginable to most. Black men and women are offered admission to prestigious colleges and universities at far lower levels of achievement than are required of others.

We also have a burgeoning Hispanic population in this country. Two generations ago, admittedly, this much smaller segment was treated poorly, denied political and legal rights, and exploited in a serious way . . . but times have changed. Throughout the nation, politicians court the Hispanic vote; and Hispanics are a presence in the Cabinet, in Congress, in executive suites, and in the media in a huge way.

Asians were used as coolies 150 years ago and treated as subhuman—now they're the key scientists, entrepreneurs, physicians, and financiers of our country. They're so dominant at our major universities that they'll clearly be even more of a factor in the nation's future than they are today.

As for Arabs in America, they too are in a rapidly burgeoning position in our society. There are powerful Arab American businessmen (including the former head of the Ford Motor Company), Arabs in the cabinet (Energy Secretary Spencer Abraham), and Arabs in high positions in the military (General John Abizaid, commander of U.S. forces in Iraq). The generation that once drove cabs and ran small shops is giving way to one that will rise to become the much-despised wealthy rulers of this country.

This is the true Rainbow Nation dreamed of by Martin Luther King, Jr. It's happening right now, this minute, in real life. If we [the authors of this book] repeat these boasts, it's because the moral accomplishment of the dismantling of institutional racism in America is a staggering event, and it wasn't won cheaply. It doesn't deserve to be despised, mocked, or belittled—it's such a triumph that it deserves to be noted over and over again.

But to hear the haters tell it, nothing has changed since the days of the Ku Klux Klan and the night riders. To hear the likes of Al Gore speak, you'd think that American schools were never integrated, White Citizens' Councils ruled the nation, and black people were as segregated and discriminated against as they were in apartheid South Africa—and other nonwhite minorities are treated in similar fashion.

Again, if the editorialists at Aljazeera could have written the script, it probably wouldn't have been terribly different.

America, the Land of Economic Exploitation

One can also look at the Left's analysis of America as an economic entity and find that here, too, the examination and conclusions are oddly similar to those coming from caves in Afghanistan. Fanatical Islamists see America as a creature of the plutocracy (especially the Jewish plutocracy, of course), bent on plundering the whole world and especially the Middle East for its natural resources, which feeds the cold-blooded greed of the American corporate titans dominated by New York and Tel Aviv.

By the same token, leading Democrats see America being run for the benefit of people like "Ken Lay and the boys" (according to former Vermont governor, screaming Howard Dean), as well as "Bush's other 'Benedict Arnold pals'" (in the words of John "Keep the Puck" Kerry). Corporate greed exploits the workers and wrecks the peace of mind of the laboring masses, especially where health care is concerned. The "fact" that so many millions of Americans lack private health-care insurance is cited as evidence that the U.S. has no moral right to fight against terrorism—which is a strange logical chain that's tricky to understand.

Is the problem economic exploitation? Is America really a society of a few wealthy users riding on the backs of a vast army of serflike laborers? Hardly. The truth is that while our country has a fantastic number of rich families, in the past 50 years almost *everyone* has gotten richer. In terms of real family wages, real purchasing power, and real housing available to Americans, the achievements of the past half century are monumental. Yes, the rich are definitely richer; but the non-rich are also much richer than they were, and richer than anyone has ever been in other countries.

You'd never know it to hear the leftists in this country talk. One might believe we were in a period of major economic oppression if we just listened to Rev. Al Sharpton or Sen. John Edwards (D-NC), whose analysis corresponds closely to that of our enemies overseas. If someone from outer space were to listen to the economic analysis of the freest, most open, most prosperous society in the world from America's bitterest enemies or from Rep. Dennis Kucinich (D-OH), a nutty little former candidate for President, he could hardly tell the difference.

By all historical measurements, America is a tolerant, open, welcoming, nurturing society that has generally acted in a magnanimous and beneficent way to the world at large and most especially to its own people. One of your authors is mindful of a conversation with his father, Herbert Stein, several years ago. After a discussion of just how good life was for the Steins, a mere two generations after three of the author's grandparents had escaped from Europe, he said, "Life for the Jewish people has never been as good anywhere or at any time as it is in America right now."

To which his father replied, "Life for *every* kind of American—Jewish, Protestant, Catholic, man, woman, black, white, Hispanic, or Asian—has never been as good anywhere as it is in America right now."

The data show this to be overwhelmingly true, as we'll demonstrate in this book. Yet how does the Left respond? With an unending litany of complaint and criticism of the nation, its institutions, and its leaders—criticism that's often floating in thin air. Now, some might say that this is politics and the "outs" always criticize the "ins." True enough—when the GOP was out of power, it certainly attacked the policies and the ethics of the Democrats (with some justification, we might add). But today's complaints, in wartime, go far beyond typical electioneering—they explicitly wallow in the politics of hate.

Hating America

In a word, there's a sustained assault against America, *by* Americans, accompanying the one by the people who incinerated the World Trade Center (although certainly not in any way overtly coordinated with those people). There's a dismaying and ongoing war against the U.S. going on day by day—a crypto-Civil War that's being fought in classrooms, on TV screens, and in our legislature. It isn't being waged by Confederates in gray and butternut uniforms, but by well-groomed (and sometimes not-so-well-groomed) men and women paid for by inheritances, foundation grants, the astronomical salaries of Hollywood, and the U.S. Congress.

This phenomenon hasn't been seen in America since the Civil War. Even the bitterness of Vietnam was less personal. It's a startling turn of events. One has to go back to Americans calling Abe Lincoln an "ape" and a "baboon" (sadly enough, the words come from General George McClellan, once the commanding general of most of the Union Army) to find such derision of an American President by respectable political figures in wartime. But the Civil War's bitterness can be understood if not condoned: Brother was fighting brother, and even justices of the Supreme Court were known to believe that secession was permissible and that slavery was lawful and sanctified by the Constitution. This was evil, but it was understandable in the context of the times, when racism was a fact of life at every level of the society.

But as far as your authors are aware, there has never been a time, after foreign aggressors attacked the United States, when respected political figures turned their rage against America and not against the people who did the attacking. Why? Why is the Left so angry at America and her rulers while the country is under attack?

This is a frightening mystery. The premise of this book is that there's something not quite rational about the level of anger directed against the United States and its Republican political leadership by much of the Left. Nothing in the real world justifies so much rage. Looked at objectively (well, as objectively as we can, since there are limits to the objectivity of anyone), something is deeply askew here.

On the one hand, we seem to have an America that stands on historical moral ground at a surpassingly elevated level. This is an America that has shown the whole world the path to freedom and prosperity. For more than a century, this country has been the magnet for all the oppressed peoples of the world who wanted to come to a new, free place to better their lives. This is the nation that, in half a century, wiped out institutionalized racism, progress unheard of and unmatched in world history. It made those who were the least among us the most among us, made the last first, and opened the doors of achievement to everyone: man and woman, black and white, Jew and Gentile, rich and poor.

This is the America that has fought two world wars and has taken no more territory in the lands we freed than the space needed to bury our dead. Quite recently, this is the America that invested its time, money, and blood in saving the Muslims of the Balkan states.

And this is the same America that was attacked so cruelly and murderously by Muslim fanatics.

Surely, the people of the United States would be satisfied by our moral and material accomplishments and would be justified at feeling real anger at our enemies—and certainly this anger and self-assertion would spread to every corner of the nation, right?

No. Instead, we have a large segment of the American population, especially on the Left, who respond to an attack on America with sympathy for the attackers and contempt for the victims. Why? What has America done to deserve this much anger from its chattering classes and major political figures? What are America's sins that deserve such retribution?

Where Will It Lead?

The authors of this book are seriously concerned about where so much anger will lead. As we see the blistering hatred aimed at America by the Left in this country, we can't help but think of how angry both sides got before the Civil War. The fury directed against President Bush and the Republican party today is eerily reminiscent of what the slave-holding state senators and representatives directed toward the abolitionists and the people who wanted to restrict the expansion of slavery to the new states and territories. And, to be fair, today's hatred is also evocative of what the abolitionists and their allies felt toward the slave holders and their allies.

This anger manifested itself in extremely sharp dialogue, but also in violence on a large scale in Kansas and in a small rebellion in Virginia. Yet this simmering bitterness didn't continue to simmer indefinitely—eventually, it burst into full boil. The murderous heat of that boil was the beginning of the Civil War, still the greatest catastrophe in American history.

The long-running rage against the nation (especially by the South) had deadly consequences: Six hundred thousand dead out of a population of 25 million, and the wounding and maiming of millions more. This would be the equivalent of seven million dead in an America of today's size—in other words, it was a horrifying loss by any standard.

Your authors are gripped by the terror that the anger of today's American leftists will lead to something horrifying as well. It seems unlikely that it would be another Civil War (although in a way we're already in a Civil War of words); a more likely and potentially equally bloody sequel to today's anger from the Left would be a failure to adequately wage the war on terror.

We're only at the beginning of a generational fight against people who would willingly destroy us; therefore, America is going to have to act unilaterally and preemptively over a sustained period to protect its citizens. However, some in the left wing have poisoned the wellsprings of patriotism that normally would sustain us over such a lengthy and costly battle. The direct consequence could be the survival and blossoming of a terrorist net able to cause truly devastating harm to the U.S. and our people, possibly even far beyond the horror of 9/11. Because America was hindered in tracking down and destroying terrorist networks, those nets might be able to use nuclear or chemical weapons against our country, with horrifying effects. This is our fear.

But we have another concern, which in some way can't be foretold right now (and who could have foretold Antietam or Gettysburg or Franklin or Cold Harbor or Sailor's Creek in 1850?): that the U.S. will simply be torn apart by the endless barrage of criticism from the Left. One might say that the ability to be self-critical, in a nation and in an individual, is a good thing, but to be endlessly self-flagellating is not. By such means, the legitimacy of the nation can be wrecked, and our future put in question. We believe that this is a consummation devoutly to be avoided.

The Plan

And so, we wrote this book. Our goal is to do the following:

1. Examine the nature of the Left's criticism of the U.S. in several areas.

2. Compare that with the real facts about what America is.

3. Offer what we hope is an original contribution: an exploration of what makes the people who bitterly criticize America so angry at her in terms of their psychological makeup—that is, we'll try to explain the psychogenesis of the anti-American Americans. Since we believe that such anger isn't justified by the facts of life in America but may instead be explained by the mental state of the haters, we'll attempt to explore what that state is. (We caution strongly that this part of the book is mostly hypothesis.)

4. Present a program for those who still love America to protect and preserve her. This is a plan for the patriotic American who believes in his or her heart that he or she has an obligation to protect the nation and the Constitution that has been so good to us all. It doesn't require that one run for Congress, raise large sums of money, or don a uniform and pick up an M16—instead, it takes activism, devotion, imagination, and a good dose of persistence . . . and a sizable amount of faith.

Now, please bear in mind a few thoughts about what this book does *not* do or say. We recognize that there are men and women on the other side of our issues with whom we disagree, yet they aren't bad people. We certainly think that they're deeply mistaken in some of what they do or say, but we don't consider them to be traitors—nor do we think that they're in the pay of al-Qaeda or the Baathists. Even people with whom we have the most basic of disagreements, and whose positions we think are desperately harmful, can be mistaken and still not be evil or wicked people. One of your authors, Ben Stein, has spent most of his adult life toiling in Hollywood. He's known many men and women whose views made him queasy, but he's not sure that he's known any who deserve to be thought of as "disloyal."

Norman Lear, for example, is the dean of Hollywood liberals. We can't help but disagree with everything (or almost everything) his People for the American Way has done, especially their attempts to block GOP judicial nominations. We think those efforts are harmful to the life and future of the nation—but we'd never say that Norman Lear is anything but sincere or well intentioned in his work. Mr. Lear flew 50 bombing missions over occupied Europe in World War II, so it's impossible to call him anything but a great citizen, despite our desperate differences with him on matters of policy.

Likewise, one of your authors has debated many times with Al Franken (the comedian and very successful author who's also an angry and sometimes cruel commentator on the Bush administration) on positions that we think are of basic importance to America. But Mr. Franken has been on four fatiguing and sometimes dangerous USO tours to entertain the troops—it's very difficult indeed to call him anything but a concerned and patriotic citizen.

On the other hand, there are some whose behavior has taken them beyond the pale into ignominy. Take, for example, Al Gore: His efforts to create racial strife in a nation that has already suffered more than enough of this are disgraceful, and as a high federal officer, he should know better. And John Kerry's rage at the plutocracy, as the husband of one of the wealthiest women in the world, is more than a bit repellent.

Still, this book is about principles rather than personalities. We didn't write it to attack or hurt any individual, but to lay out a basic threat to our nation and to our children and grandchildren: that of a division based on some sort of perceptual disorder, which may be to the 21st century what the Civil War's origins were to the 19th. We must pray that it doesn't happen, but we must also recall what a distinguished Democrat said 42 years ago: John F. Kennedy said that we must pray for the Almighty to do what we think is best. Yet we must also and always recognize that here on earth, God's work must truly be our own. If we're to ensure that America survives, then the last, best hope of mankind is up to us.

★★★ ★★★

The U.S. Economy

"Today, under George W. Bush, there are two Americas, not one: One America that does the work, another America that reaps the reward. One America that pays the taxes, another America that gets the tax breaks. One America that will do anything to leave its children a better life, another America that never has to do a thing because its children are already set for life. One America—middle-class America—whose needs Washington has long forgotten, another America—narrow-interest America—whose every wish is Washington's command. One America that is struggling to get by, another America that can buy anything it wants, even a Congress and a President."
— Senator John Edwards ("The Breck Girl")

"George Bush's failed economic plan gave us another year of lower incomes and higher poverty rates—as if we needed more evidence that the Bush administration's economic policies have failed Americans. For two and a half years, George Bush sat on his hands while hard-working middle-class Americans suffer

through job loss, reduced wages, and increased costs for health care and college. Middle-class families are hurting and need relief."
— Senator John Kerry

"Today the large organization is lord and master, and most of its employees have been desensitized much as were the medieval peasants who never knew they were serfs."
— Ralph Nader (whom we actually like in some ways . . .)

"Each year an estimated 30 million Americans go hungry."
— Cynthia Bowers, CBS Evening News, July 10, 2003

"The Agriculture Department figures one out of six children in America faces hunger; that's more than 12 million kids."
— Scott Pelley, 60 Minutes II, January 8, 2003

According to the media, the U.S. economy is a cold-hearted machine that enriches the few and exploits the many. Turn on the TV news, and every economic event becomes the subject for a Marxist critique on the dysfunctional state of capitalism in America. The rich, true to form, keep getting richer, while the poor suffer in Dickensian destitution. Thanks to free trade, factories are closing, and our good jobs are being shipped abroad, consigning the workers left behind to low-wage service jobs—if they can find jobs at all. The middle class is disintegrating, and now Mom and Dad must both labor to bring in what Dad alone could earn a generation ago. For the poor, homelessness is rampant; and the quality of life for all Americans is in irreversible decline. Very likely, all this is the fault of the failed policies of George W. Bush and his Republican henchmen.

Sure, this sounds familiar, but is it even remotely true? Let's examine the facts in this chapter.

Poverty in America

Any poverty in a country as rich as the U.S. is deeply unfortunate. But how bad is it really in America today? A little digging beneath the liberal news machinery is instructive. So is a little history.

In 1937, Franklin Roosevelt could look out to see "one-third of a nation ill-housed, ill-clad, ill-nourished." Our image of the poor in America stems from the haunting photographs from that era: people who don't have enough to eat, who wear rags, and who live in squalor, their faces pinched with desperation. But does this accurately depict the condition of the poor in this country today? Hardly. Consider the following, as applied to the 35 million people in America classified as living in poverty by the Census Bureau in 2003:

Food

Here is our first clue that something has gone very wrong with the statisticians in Washington. In other countries, the primary health problem of the poor is malnutrition; in America, it's obesity. Twenty-six percent of those living below the poverty line are obese, according to the Centers for Disease Control and Prevention. Never before have so many people who can't afford enough to eat been so overweight. Our underprivileged children today are supernourished, which is why, astonishingly, they grow up to be an inch taller and ten pounds heavier than the average kid did 50 years ago. According to the Department of Agriculture, 97 percent of the U.S. population lives in families that reported they had "enough food to eat" during 2002. Still, half of one percent said that they "often" didn't have enough to eat due to lack of funds. This is heartbreaking and needs to be addressed, but it's almost certainly the smallest percentage of people in such dire straits in any large nation in history. *That's* the news flash, not the "Two Americas" of Senator Edwards's imagination.

Clothing

The American Enterprise Institute's Michael Novak grew up in a poor family, where he often had to wear hand-me-down tennis shoes with holes in them. When he visits poor neighborhoods today, he notices what people are wearing on their feet as a tell-tale indicator of how they're doing economically. What does he see? People wearing $200 athletic shoes. To be sure, we don't allege that all poor people wear expensive shoes, or that even if they did, that would mean they're undeserving of help. But the fact is (thanks largely to free trade), in the last 40 years the price of clothing in America has fallen by half as a percentage of family budgets. This means that, except for the most abject homeless people, shabby or even unfashionable clothing is rare indeed these days.

Shelter

Fully 46 percent of households classified as "poor" own their own homes, which have three bedrooms, one and a half baths, a garage, and a porch or patio on average. According to Robert Rector and Kirk Johnson's 2004 Heritage Foundation Report, "Understanding Poverty In America," these domiciles have more square footage available per person than does the typical (that is, non-poor) resident of London or Paris.

Health Care

Poor Americans receive free medical care thanks to Medicaid. Far from being a bare-bones policy, Medicaid covers such procedures as biofeedback, impotence treatment, sex-change operations, computerized tomography, and even obesity treatment. A glance at a recent "Medicaid Coverage—What's New" Webpage reveals that they're planning to add the following treatments: magnetic resonance spectroscopy for brain tumors, radioimmunotherapy for non-Hodgkin's lymphoma, oxaliplatin and irinotecan for colorectal cancer, ocular photodynamic therapy with verteporfin for macular degeneration, and FDG Positron Emission Tomography and other neuroimaging devices for suspected dementia. Were these treatments available even to billionaires 25 years ago?

Education

Free elementary and high school education is, of course, provided throughout the U.S. But students from poor backgrounds who want to continue on to college can apply for some $3.5 billion in need-based scholarships that were given away by state universities in 2000 to 2001, to take the figures from the latest year for which they were available. Looking at all types of scholarships from both public and private schools, these totaled over $13 billion in 1995 to 1996 (the last year figures were available). Clearly, the tools for self-improvement are there for anyone who wants to make use of them.

While the condition of people living in poverty today is undoubtedly far from ideal, poverty isn't what it used to be. It's nothing like Depression-era poverty or even the poverty of the 1960s, when so many baby boomers developed their social consciences. And there's now a substantial question about just how bad poverty was, except in some concentrated areas, in the '60s.

Rating the "Poverty Rate"

In 1965, President Lyndon Johnson launched the mother of all tax-and-spend government programs under the banner of a "war on poverty." (Johnson is alleged to have said at the time, "I'll have them n——s voting Democratic for the next 200 years," according to Ronald Kessler's *Inside the White House*.) His administration created an index called the "poverty rate" to justify its massive campaign of income redistribution.

Here's how they did it. Civil servant Molly Orshansky took a 1955 finding that Americans spent one-third of their income on food, then went to the Department of Agriculture to ask how much their 1961 "thrifty food plan" cost to follow. If the cheapest nutritionally adequate menu cost a certain amount, and the price of food equaled one-third of people's income, then people who didn't earn at least three times that amount must be living in poverty. Either they were going without needed food, or they were cutting back on shelter or clothing in order to survive. Obviously, this was an extremely crude measurement, not allowing for the benefits of owned or subsidized housing or transportation, for example.

Having established this poverty rate, they proceeded to adjust it every year for inflation using the Consumer Price Index, which allowed them to make a running estimate of how many among us were living in poverty.

The poverty rate was a flawed statistic from the outset, and those flaws have just been magnified over time. In the first place, the cost of food as a percentage of people's incomes has declined dramatically since 1955: People today spend closer to 10 percent of their discretionary income on food, including eating in restaurants, according to the Department of Agriculture. (The Bureau of Labor Statistics says that people in the lowest income class spend 17 percent of their total expenditures on food.) On top of this, most economists believe that the Consumer Price Index (CPI), by which the poverty rate is annually rejiggered, overstates inflation by about one percentage point per year—which tends to add up after 30 years, artificially tripping more and more people over the poverty line.

As a result, the number of Americans living under the poverty line in 2002 was even greater (12.1 percent of individuals, or about 7 percent of families) than it was in 1973 (11.1 percent of individuals), even though the per capita gross domestic product (GDP) adjusted for inflation—a reasonable measure of quality of life in a society—was more than 35 percent higher. Since the poverty rate has never been adjusted for real improvements in our standard of living, it's a dubious statistic for comparing the poor of today with the poor of yesterday.

Nicholas Eberstadt of the Harvard Center for Population and Developmental Studies thinks that the real problem with the poverty rate is that it measures the wrong thing: income, rather than consumption. Daniel Slesnick of the University of Texas agrees, writing in *Living Standards in the United States* that "there is little basis in economic theory for using income as a measure of welfare. As a snapshot estimate of the standard of living, the consumption of goods and services is of paramount importance."

In other words, people aren't necessarily poor when their income is low; they're poor when they can't buy the things they need—two conditions that aren't necessarily the same. The poor today spend between two and three dollars for every dollar they earn, which is why looking at consumption patterns suggests a very different picture of those supposedly living in poverty.

* * *

How can the poor spend so much more than they earn? Well, this is actually less mysterious than it seems. The Heritage Foundation's Robert Rector notes that the Census Bureau's annual report on income and poverty in America (which the press invariably seizes upon for whatever bad news they can pluck out of it) omits many types of cash and non-cash income, including a half-trillion dollars of government aid to the underprivileged and elderly such as Medicaid, food stamps, and public housing. Many of the people who appear poor in terms of income are retirees living off their savings, or full-time students with other sources of revenue.

From a consumption point of view, the price of essentials has come down, leaving impoverished people with more discretionary income for other kinds of goods and services. The proportion of total consumption that poor Americans devote to food, shelter, and clothing has fallen since the 1970s, from 52 to 37 percent. In *Myths of Rich & Poor*, W. Michael Cox and Richard Alm point out that a basket of groceries that cost nine hours of labor to buy in 1920 takes us only an hour and 45 minutes to earn today. One hundred kilowatt hours of electricity took a half hour of labor to earn in 1960, but it takes less than half that time today. All of this means that it takes the poor fewer hours at work to cover their basic requirements for food, clothing, and shelter.

Poverty Is a Temporary Condition

To see how looking at the poor through the lens of consumption instead of income shifts the analysis, consider Slesnick's analysis: In 1995, 14 percent of the population was classified as "poor" according to the Census's *Statistical Abstract of the United States.* Moving to a consumption-based analysis drops this figure to 9 percent. Correcting for the bias in the CPI further lowers this rate to 7 percent. Between 1 and 4 percent of the population appears to be intractably poor by current standards, although they're doing well by global standards—and by historical standards of poverty within the United States. Again, any is too many, but this is far from a huge percentage of the nation. It's very far indeed from the "Two Americas" reported by Senator Edwards.

Moreover, for most, the average stay below the poverty line lasts just over four months. According to the Census Bureau, only about one-third of those in poverty at any given time will stay there for two years. This isn't perfection, but neither is it the Democratic party image. (That is, the image they project when running against Republicans. An interesting fact is that the "poverty rate" stays about the same year to year no matter who's running the country, yet the Democrats only notice it when the GOP is in office.)

The real problem with the "poor" in America is mostly not about money, in any case, but about moral and social behaviors that are dangerous and unhealthy. As the economist Herbert Stein (father of co-author Ben Stein) noted in *The Wall Street Journal* shortly before his death in 1999:

> What makes poverty in America unlovely to me is not only a low level of income. It is the association of that condition with a high probability of being either a crime victim or

a criminal, of attending an unsafe and disorderly school, of living in an atmosphere of drug and alcohol abuse and, most of all, of not having a supportive spouse or two caring parents. All people with low incomes do not have these problems, and some with higher incomes do have them. But the association of these problems with lowness of income is close enough to describe the condition of poverty that I find unlovely. That condition deserves, in my opinion, our most intensive care. I believe that the present focus on inequality of income diverts national attention from it.

Of course it's bad to be poor in America, but it's not quite the streets of Calcutta (and, as we shall see, the streets of Calcutta are no longer the streets of Calcutta either, thanks to globalization). We need to do everything we can to help those who are down-and-out, but it must be acknowledged that some people by their own actions place themselves beyond the reach of help. Living in poverty today is largely the result of specific unfortunate life choices that people make. The 2001 census data suggest that your chance of being poor in the United States is statistically negligible provided you do three things: (1) Complete high school, (2) marry and stay married, and (3) take a full-time job, even at minimum wage. If you're married, you won't have children out of wedlock, another lifestyle option that tends to lead to a dead-end street of poverty. The National Longitudinal Survey of Youth study found that children raised by never-married mothers were nine times more likely to live in poverty than children raised by two parents married to each other.

Poverty is a terrible thing, and we don't dispute or belittle it. But it isn't even remotely the problem that it was in the Great Depression or that it's made to seem by Democrats who want Republicans' jobs. It needs sober attention—mostly by individuals—and hysteria helps no one but office seekers.

The New Lower Class

To be in the lowest-income quintile (the poorest one-fifth of the total population) in 2002, a family had to make less than $24,000 a year. This bar has been raised 16 percent since 1980, when it was $20,693 in constant dollars. According to the 1996 report of the President's Council of Economic Advisers, the *average* income inside this quintile declined by 15 percent between 1979 and 1993.

As horrible as that sounds, it doesn't necessarily mean that the income of any person who was in the bottom fifth declined. As Herbert Stein wrote: "Suppose that in 1979 the bottom fifth consisted half of female-headed families with average incomes of $10,000 and half of male-headed families with average incomes of $20,000, so that the average for the whole group was $15,000. Then, suppose that between 1979 and 1993 the real income of each type of family rises by 10 percent, but that now instead of 50 percent being headed by females it is 84 percent. Then the average income of the group will be $12,760, a decline of roughly 15 percent."

In other words, unless we know a great deal more about who's in that group and what happened to them, the statistic is malleable and subject to artifactual distortions. If a million immigrants just jumped the border to join the poorest fifth, and they earn $5,000 today compared to $1,000 in their native countries, their income has increased fivefold. However, the net effect would be to drag down the overall income of this country's bottom fifth—even while it raised the incomes of those individuals within the group proportionately.

Today, the lowest-income quintile no longer consists of a dad who works full-time but can't make ends meet; instead, it's now primarily made up of young single mothers and older widows—most of whom don't work full-time. Contrast this to most married families, in which both the husband and wife work (and often full-time)—and their combined incomes put them in a higher-income bracket. The net effect is to squeeze more single heads of households into the lowest income group.

The Census uses the household as its unit of measurement, yet not all households are the same size. Lower-income households, for example, are smaller than their upper-income counterparts—so because their income is distributed among fewer people, each individual member is proportionately that much better off.

Another important fact about those in the lowest quintile of earnings in the United States is that their residence on the "Mediterranean Avenue" end of America's Monopoly board is likely to be short-lived. According to the University of Michigan's Panel Study of Income Dynamics, America is a highly upwardly mobile society. Only about one-third of Americans in the lowest quintile find themselves there a decade later—the rest move on up to higher incomes. Only 5 percent of those in the bottom income quintile in 1975 were still there in 1991, whereas nearly 30 percent had moved to the highest income quintile. Academic estimates suggest that a person's chances of exiting the lowest quintile within a year are in the 20 to 40 percent range. While, historically, most societies have been caste-based and afforded little opportunity for personal advancement, contemporary America is a meritocracy. Most of the downward mobility in the U.S. is by people in the top quintile, who must make way for new entrants.

★ ★ ★

Most statistics about income also overlook the fact that it varies significantly over a lifetime. Many of those in the lowest quintile are youths entering the workforce in their first McJob, from which they can be expected to graduate before long. Most people tend to go into the workforce at entry-level wages, grow in their careers (often switching jobs several times) until they hit their peak earnings in their 40s and 50s. Then, in their 60s, they pull back, and incomes drop after retirement. As *The American Enterprise's* Karl Zinsmeister puts it, "Who is 'rich' and who is 'poor' tends to be predominantly a question of life-stage in this country. Most people cycle through different zones of the income spectrum at different times, depending on whether they are raising children, are in college, are part of a couple with two paychecks, are retirees living on investments, whatever. Americans change jobs a lot. They move across the country. They divorce at grievously high rates. In a year when one of these things happens, the household income may tumble. But over the long haul, prosperous mobility is the norm."

Here's another excursion into the land of questionable statistics: The Census data that newspapers and politicians use to divide rich and poor only look at pretax income. This fails to take into account the equalizing effects of taxation, which fall largely on the upper class. The top 5 percent of taxpayers pay 56 percent of our income taxes. It's not all weekends in Gstaad for the rich—they create and operate businesses that hire the rest of us and pay our salaries. They also donate most of the money that goes to charity and medical research: In 2000, the top 400 taxpayers donated 7 percent of all the charitable gifts reported on income tax by themselves. The rich also act as an important counterweight to the progressive encroachment of government in everyone's lives.

How bad are conditions for the poor in America today? A little vignette makes this point: Both of your authors grew up in the suburbs during the 1950s, yet neither of our homes had air-conditioning, despite the sweltering summer temperatures outside. (Today, two-thirds of households classified as "poor" have air-conditioning.) In addition, our black-and-white TV sets received a few local channels via "rabbit ears," broadcast by stations that were on the air from six in the morning until midnight. If we wanted to see a movie that had left the local theaters, well, there really was no way to do so. Today, 97 percent of the poor families in the United States have color TVs (half of them have *two*); 78 percent own VCRs or DVD players; and 62 percent get cable or satellite TV.

When we called Grandma long-distance in the '50s, it was a big event. We had to talk fast, because phone rates were 30 times higher than they are today. Airline travel back then was a luxury for the rich, or the "jet set," as they'd soon be called. Our family cars didn't have anti-lock brake systems, air bags, or stereo FM radios with CD players; nor did they boast cup holders, sunroofs, anti-theft devices, or cruise control. More than 70 percent of poor households today have one or more cars, and while these vehicles may not have all of the above features, remember that cars in the '50s didn't even come equipped with seat belts to protect passengers from the metal dashboards and glass windshields in front of their faces.

Twenty-five percent of poor families had personal computers in 2001 (no doubt a much higher percentage does today), each of which probably contains more total computing power than existed in the entire country in the '50s, when it took a computer the size of a room to play a game of tic-tac-toe.

Today, the average American poor person lives better than the middle-class G.I. returning from World War II did, and better than 80 percent of the world's population does now. No wonder so many immigrants are willing to risk their lives in dangerous gambits just to arrive on our shores and live in so-called poverty here. A life of impoverishment by U.S. standards is an American dream to most of the rest of the world. In California, where one-fourth of the population (including the governor) is foreign-born, a large percentage of the immigrants start out poor (25 percent in 1980), but after 20 years, nearly 90 percent of them have reached the middle class.

Bush and the Economy

> *"The economic policies of George W. Bush are the worst*
> *in our nation's history."*
> — **Senator John Kerry**

It will come as a surprise to some to learn that President Bush and the Republican party aren't the cause of poverty in America today. According to the Council of Economic Advisers, the latest recession began in the fourth quarter of 2000, when Clinton was still President. There is dispute on this point, and as of this writing, the National Bureau of Economic Research still says that the recession began six weeks after Bush took office. Still, during what was supposedly the economy's "golden age," the stock market began to crash, economic growth slowed, and the cracks in the boom of 1998 and 1999 began to show. So, by definition, and by economic fact, President Clinton couldn't possibly have left a legacy of a solid economy to President Bush or there wouldn't have been a recession.

The economy didn't change from rock solid on January 20, 2001, at 11:59 A.M. to falling apart at noon when President Bush took his oath. All the preconditions for the slide in 2001 were already present, including the fallout from the biggest, most poorly regulated stock-market bubble in history, the effects of an unparalleled inventory bubble in high tech that was already in place in 2000, and the effect of the fiscal drag of the Clinton administration's running surpluses that were far larger than the perilous state of the economy warranted. Large surpluses slow down an economy, say some experts, and the only variable is how long the lag time is between the surpluses and the slow-down. What Bush inherited was an economy that was poised to slow down, and by a lot. This would have been the fate of Al Gore's economy if he'd won in 2000 as well—and it wouldn't have been his fault either.

Governments basically have two ways to fight recession: monetary policy and fiscal policy. Monetary policy is set by the Federal Reserve Board (or "the Fed"), which isn't controlled by the President; but in any event, the Fed did what it could to temper the recession: monetary easing, money creation, and setting low short- and long-term interest rates. Fiscal policy, however, is set by the President and Congress. Bush has cut taxes and increased spending, both Economics 101 measures for dealing with a recession. When government sees persistent economic weakness, it turns to deficit spending to pump things up, standard operating procedure since the latter days of FDR. There's nothing further to be done, and the data to date suggest that the Bush economic policies are working well. The economy is reviving quickly from the slowdown.

As we write this book, productivity is rising at unprecedented rates. Corporate profits—most owned by the pension funds of America's workers—are at an all-time high. It's true that unemployment, especially in manufacturing, remains elevated, but this is generally agreed upon by those with no close friends running for office to have nothing to do with Bush's policies. It's an artifact of large increases in productivity and a worldwide movement to free trade that has been the policy of both parties for many years. Short of returning to a protectionism that would be ruinous, there's nothing that Bush, Kerry, or anyone else can do about it until the workers from manufacturing are absorbed into the service sector.

The truth is that Bush inherited a dicey economic situation, mainly the fallout from the stock-market and high-tech bubbles. This was hugely compounded by the effects of 9/11 terrorism. Now, President Bush doesn't want a weak economy—he wants a powerful, job-creating one as any patriot would, be they Democrat or Republican, and he's using the tools he has available to secure this outcome. How he can be blamed for economic facts that he didn't cause, especially when he's done every reasonable thing he could do to resist them, is a mystery. People aren't generally considered to be responsible for effects they neither caused nor allowed to happen by negligence . . . and this should apply to elected officials of either party.

It may well be that the tax cuts Bush proposed on upper-income Americans are too large. But the mechanism by which this would cause a recession is at present unknown.

The Non-Disappearing Middle Class

During the Clinton administration, Labor Secretary Robert Reich wrote in *The Washington Times* that "the growth in inequality and the precariousness of the middle class are stunningly obvious features of the contemporary American landscape." On the campaign trail last year, Senator Edwards echoed that theme: "Middle-class families have gone from being able to save for retirement or buy a house, to now teetering on the edge of bankruptcy." Senator Kerry seconded that emotion, claiming, "With George Bush in the White House, the middle class has been forgotten all over again."

Is the middle class in fact disappearing, as America bifurcates into a master-slave society of rich and poor? In a word, no. The middle class is far more prosperous by every statistical measurement—income, housing, quality of life, and education. As we've stated before, the rich are getting richer, but so is everyone else in the U.S. The 5 percent of Americans who have fallen out of middle-class income ranks have primarily done so by moving into the upper-middle class. (Not a bad way to "fall.") The real reason the middle class seems to be disappearing is that most Americans' lives have improved to such a degree that they can no longer remember what it was like to be middle class, even in the prosperous 1950s.

Although wage growth has slowed from about 2.6 percent in the postwar era to 1.6 percent in the last quarter of the century, this ignores the contribution of fringe benefits to total compensation. These have expanded dramatically, thanks to a tax code that doesn't directly tax benefits and so increases their value to employees over ordinary income. Today's workers often receive health insurance, dental and vision benefits, maternity and paternity leave, stock options, and matching contributions to their retirement plans—a whole list of goodies that earlier generations of workers did not. All this is missed by statistical measurements that focus on income alone.

Here's a stunning piece of data: Per capita consumption in America has roughly tripled from the end of World War II up to today. According to the World Bank, this country's real per capita GDP, which increased 39-fold since 1789 and more than 8-fold since 1900, has approximately doubled since 1970.

Some would claim that this explosion of prosperity belies a sad economic fact: Whereas back in the good old days Mom stayed home to raise the kids, now Dad's salary has fallen to the point where Mom has to dump the kids in day care and go to work, too, just to make ends meet.

This is less tragic than it sounds. Yesterday's stay-at-home mom wasn't just filing her nails—she was cooking, sewing, cleaning, shopping, and shuffling the kids to school, baseball games, haircuts, and piano lessons. This was hard work, which is why many women today are thrilled to subcontract it out, put on their suits, and head into the job market. If Mom can earn $50,000 a year as a sales rep or $100,000 as an attorney, it makes little economic sense for her to spend her time ironing or folding clothes (unless she derives a great deal of emotional fulfillment from these activities). Instead, she can hire others who specialize in these tasks to do them full-time—people who are probably more than happy to do them compared with what they would have been doing in Guatemala.

The "Harriet Nelson" moms of yesteryear spent hours on shopping and food preparation every day, as going out to eat was a rarity. Today, microwaving prepared food or getting carryout from a restaurant is the norm, while the home-cooked meal pre-pared from scratch has become a luxury. When Mom is a brain surgeon and Dad is head of North American sales, homemade lasagna has an implied labor cost of several thousand dollars (in other words, what Mom and Dad could have earned if they'd spent the time at work instead of in the kitchen). No wonder we get takeout.

Despite what we read in the lifestyle section of the local newspaper, middle-class Americans are also far richer than ever before when it comes to another finite commodity: leisure time. We enter the workforce later, retire earlier, and have more time off than any society has hitherto enjoyed. In 1870, the average employed U.S. worker logged about 3,000 hours of work per year; by the 1990s, this had fallen to 1,600 hours. American workers have gained five extra years of waking leisure time since 1973 alone. And this isn't just time tacked on at the beginning and end of their work lives: The average adult woman spent 4.7 more hours per week on leisure pursuits in 1995 than she did in 1965, while the average adult male gained 7.9 hours of recreation per week in the same period (according to John Robinson of the University of Maryland and Geoffrey Godbey of the University of Pennsylvania). Likewise, in 1919, only 152,000 Americans enjoyed travel abroad, but in 1997, some 24 million did. One glance at the enormous expansion of the leisure, recreation, and entertainment industries in the past decade gives lie to the idea that we're all working harder than ever before.

Living the Good Life

The average middle-class person in the United States today lives like a king . . . actually, better than any king of yore—better than Caesar, better than Napoleon, and better than the Rockefellers or Carnegies or Vanderbilts in the 1890s. Andrew Carnegie couldn't go to Paris for the weekend; he couldn't even call London to check on the stock market. He couldn't hear the Berlin Philharmonic unless he traveled to Berlin. He couldn't always get his gin and tonic with ice cubes in it, or eat watermelon on Christmas Day. He couldn't take an aspirin if he had a headache. He couldn't get Thai or Mexican or Italian or Indian takeout, and there weren't 50 flavors of coffee to drink on every street corner.

If he had a cavity (very likely, since both his drinking water and toothpaste were unfluoridated), the trip to the dentist would be unforgettable. No medicines could help him with obesity, hair loss, or erectile dysfunction; and God help him if he really became ill. There was no open-heart surgery, no anti-cancer surgery or medications, no antibiotics or antivirals; if his child developed black diphtheria, nothing could be done. Half the population back in Carnegie's day died of contagious diseases, resulting in an average life expectancy of 49 years for males. While it's difficult to put a price tag on the extra years of life a person lives today, they are worth something.

Whether out of ignorance or some sense of entitlement, we tend to see these amazing advantages of modern life as our birthright. It's easy to overlook what a cornucopia present-day America is, with its dazzling array of personal options and consumer choices almost unthinkable only a few generations ago. This is worth remembering the next time we find ourselves cursing our fate because we can't find a Wi-Fi high-speed Internet connection at the airport, or if the neighborhood grocery store is out of Diet Vanilla Coke in 12-ounce cans.

* * *

One of your authors recently went on a tour of a home built in 1950. The owner apologetically pointed out that the closets were small, adding that "there's no storage in any of these old houses." Of course, these houses had plenty of room to hold everything Americans owned at the time they were built. But now Americans have much more stuff than ever before—so much designer clothing; so many appliances, durable consumer goods, and cupboards stocked with food; so much sports and recreational gear; so many books, toys, telephones, stereos, televisions, computers, and musical instruments, that there's literally no place to put it all. Homes are now twice as big as they were in the '50s, and there's a permanent industry in America that puts additions on houses.

Compared to the mud huts and tar-paper shacks where the rest of the world lives, the typical middle-class American home looks like a cross between Santa Claus's workshop and Scrooge McDuck's Money Bin. In addition, according to the Federal Reserve's 2001 *Survey of Consumer Finances*, 85 percent of American families own a car (in fact, we own more cars than we have drivers), 68 percent own their personal residence (a number that has reached this all-time high under the fascist, repressive

Bush regime), and 52 percent own stock or mutual fund portfolios (a percentage that's doubled since 1983), with a median value of $34,300. American families have an average net worth of $395,500 and the median (50th percentile) family has a net worth of $86,100—up 40 percent since 1992 in constant dollars. More than 15 million households in America earn over $100,000 per year—nearly 18 percent of all families in the country.

Meanwhile, the top 20 percent of households had a median annual income of $72,000. At the penthouse level, Merrill Lynch estimates that there are over two million millionaires in the United States today—and that estimate doesn't even take into account the value of people's real estate. (Neither does the 2003 estimate from the NFO WorldGroup, which pegged the number of millionaire households at 3.8 million.) Add real estate to the pot, and the number of U.S. millionaires jumps to about eight million, according to *Time* magazine—about one-quarter of the entire population of Canada. This is a very rich country. The average productivity per person is approximately eight times what it was 125 years ago, creating a society of vast abundance.

America, God has truly shed His grace on thee.

Foreigners Know Best

Other countries are often held up as good economic examples for the United States to follow, but is this fair? Let's see.

Europe

"How does this sound to you: shorter working hours, longer holidays, and no pay cuts? . . . The French, they've got it right, don't they?"
— **Katie Couric,** *Today* show, August 1, 2001

Because of centralized wage setting, government restrictions on firing, and protracted unemployment benefits, workers in Europe are supposedly a happier bunch than their counterparts in the U.S. Not only that, they get to live in great cities like London and Paris and Rome—places that Americans have to spend thousands of dollars to visit on their vacation time.

Should the United States strive to emulate the more sophisticated ways of the Europeans? Decidedly not. Upon closer examination, these benefits turn out not to be benefits at all. In economics, when you raise the price of something (in this case, labor), people generally buy less of it. European companies are reluctant to hire because new employees are expensive and, once employed, are almost impossible to fire if they don't work out. Workers can become complacent, since they have little incentive to give their best performance or improve their skills.

It comes as no surprise, then, to learn that unemployment in Europe is chronically high. As of late 2003, unemployment there was 8.8 percent, compared with 5.7 percent in the U.S. Europe's state-sponsored social welfare policies only serve to protect employed workers, at the direct expense of people seeking jobs. Europeans pay for this via the lower standard of living that accompanies their more inefficient deployment of resources, which is why a significantly lower per capita gross domestic product (GDP) prevails throughout Europe compared to that of the United States. In 2002, the per capita GDP of the United Kingdom was 70 percent of ours, Finland's was 68 percent,

France and Germany's were 65 percent, Italy's was 57 percent, and Spain's was 43 percent. These countries are back where we were in the 1980s in terms of the purchasing power of their per capita GDPs. As tourists, we admire the leisurely lifestyle of today's Europeans, as well as the great achievements of their ancestors, but notice how few of us actually move there.

Japan

After World War II, Japan graduated from making paper umbrellas and transistor radios into an economic superpower. Just a decade ago, America bashers were touting Japan as the country that would make our country obsolete. As *The New York Times Magazine* wrote of Japan at the time: "The fundamental principles of this system are applicable to every industry . . . [and] will have a profound impact on human society. It will truly change the world." The secret to Japan's "economic miracle" was supposedly something Americans couldn't understand, called *kaizen*, a lean manufacturing technique involving relentless, continuous improvement. Coupled with the anthill-like mentality of the Japanese worker (in contrast to their sloppy U.S. counterparts), Japan turned into an unstoppable dynamo. U.S. corporations frantically sent executives to Japan to do tai chi at 6 A.M. on the factory floor and learn the basics of T.Q.C. (Total Quality Control). The future of our own economy looked grim, as the Japanese were devouring our national treasures like jujubes. Rumor had it that they'd already bought most of California, and with Rockefeller Center already in their portfolio, could the entire island of Manhattan be far behind? As a *New Yorker* article opined back then, pretty soon *we* might be the ones making paper umbrellas.

But it didn't happen. A big chunk of Japan, Inc., turned out to be *zaitech,* which we might translate as "creative accounting," or a system of financial engineering that inflated profits while disguising losses. The Nikkei (the Japanese stock market) swelled to nearly 40,000 in 1989, and then the bubble burst—14 years later, the Nikkei stands at 10,676. Having sold Rockefeller Center to Japan for $1.5 billion in 1989, we bought it back for $1.2 billion in 1996. In fact, it was the American system that had proved unstoppable.

The Third World

Today, we keep hearing that all the good jobs are being shipped to Mexico and Southeast Asia. Since the U.S. customer wants to pay low prices and shop at Wal-Mart, this means that manufacturing jobs must go to the low-cost provider. But how can American workers compete with third-world peasants who willingly work for a few dollars a day? Aren't we being sold down the river by greedy corporations who are only out to make a buck and don't care who gets hurt in the process? Senator John Kerry thinks he can turn this trend around: "I believe manufacturing in America can come back and shine as never before," he says. "But it won't happen with the failed policies of the past. We need a President with the courage to fight for our economic future." There are, of course, no specifics that add up—nor could there be, since the President is powerless against these forces.

Make no mistake: Losing one's job can be a shattering experience—overwhelming, devastating, depressing, lingering in its ill effects; and in a free-market economy, there's a constant, Shiva-like dance of job creation and destruction. Newspaper headlines are full of stories of plant closings, with sad human-interest sidebars and dire predictions of what lies ahead. Less often reported is that for every old job that's lost, new ones are being created.

In 1900, the leading occupation in the United States was "farmer"; today, it's "retail sales associate." While we can all be nostalgic for the days when most people worked on the family homestead, modern methods have passed today's farmer by (not to mention that farming is hard, dangerous, poorly paid work). Now the farm economy is much more productive, with far fewer workers than it once needed. A person today is incomparably better off working as a barista at Starbucks (with benefits) than laboring in a field with a mule.

Yet there are always trade-offs: It's harder to find a blacksmith, cobbler, or telegraph operator these days—we've voted with our dollars to have a different kind of lifestyle. We no longer use telephone operators to dial our phone numbers for us; we push a button on our cell phones and connect ourselves. The call goes through faster, better, and for a fraction of the cost, yet it means that we need far fewer operators than before. On the other hand, the economy has created new and more specialized jobs such as airline pilot, CAT-scan operator, and computer programmer, careers that didn't even exist a century ago. This role specialization allows us, individually and collectively, to express our comparative advantage, dramatically raising our standard of living in the process. There's just no way to stop the world at some arbitrary point in time that maintains our job forever while everyone else's moves forward.

But are we in fact shipping all the good manufacturing jobs to Taiwan while Americans are left with the crummy service jobs like flipping hamburgers and cleaning motel rooms?

The manufacturing sector is 12 percent of the private economy, and as critics have correctly pointed out, many of these jobs are the ones being exported. However, according to the Bureau of Labor Statistics, the service sector employs 80 percent of the workers in the private economy. While some of these are entry-level jobs like cooking and cleaning, the sector also includes nurses and doctors, entertainers, teachers, police officers and fire-fighters, scientists, attorneys, architects, managers, and so on. As societies evolve economically, the trend is away from working in a mine or in a factory to performing service-related work. Tom Cruise is a service worker; so is the president of Goldman Sachs. Are these bad jobs?

Critics of America's competitive capabilities are way off base. If we were really shipping all the good jobs overseas, our employment and our incomes would be falling; yet today both employment and incomes are rising. In fact, most of us are already service workers and are better off for it. We Americans have leveraged our educations and skills with technology in a competitive marketplace, and are now in the process of exporting this template to the rest of the world for the good of all. Will this have balance of trade implications? Yes, but these are too complicated and unknowable to deal with here.

The Real Picture

In conclusion, the story here is that the U.S. economy, while still subject to cyclical forces and long- term trends of productivity growth and trade effects, is incredibly strong—it's ten times the size of China's, with one-fifth of the population. It's a machine for generating unheard-of prosperity, which is true for the whole nation, even for many of the least well-off among us. The real story of America is the unprecedented wealth of the ordinary citizen; even for most of the poorest of us, life is (by historical and comparative standards) extremely good.

Or, to put it another way, the nation's critics (especially its left-wing critics), have got it backwards—as office seekers and troublemakers usually do.

★★★ ★★★

U.S. Imperialism

"Whoever attacked the World Trade Center and the Pentagon, and our sense of daily trust and freedom, must be found. But America must find itself, too. The targets clearly represented America's global power, a power that is not innocent of arrogance, either militarily or economically. With all the condolence that can be offered, it is incongruent to think that the world's leading exporter of the tools of death and destruction would not someday be visited with an evil in return."
— **Derrick Z. Jackson,** *The Boston Globe*, September 12, 2001

"Quite simply, for many workers around the world, the oppression of the unchecked commissars has been replaced by the oppression of the unregulated capitalists, who move their manufacturing from country to country, constantly in search of those who will work for the lowest wages and lowest standards. To some, the Nike swoosh is now as scary as the hammer and sickle."
— **Thomas L. Friedman,** *The New York Times*, July 30, 1999

*"Let us find a way to resist fundamentalism that leads to vio-
lence—fundamentalism of all kinds, in al-Qaeda and within
our government. . . . Our fundamentalism is business, the unfet-
tered spread of our economic interests throughout the globe.
Our resistance to this war should be our resistance to
profit at the cost of human life."*
— **Susan Sarandon,** October 26, 2002

*"This is a racist and imperialist war. The warmongers who
stole the White House (you call them 'hawks,' but I would never
disparage such a fine bird) have hijacked a nation's grief and
turned it into a perpetual war on any non-white country
they choose to describe as terrorist."*
— **Woody Harrelson,** The Guardian, October 17, 2002

*"While the end to the Saddam regime means a return to long-
denied freedoms for all Iraqis, it may also mean at least a tem-
porary rollback of some hard-won freedoms for millions of
Iraqi women. . . . While Saddam's regime brutalized women—
rape, torture, even beheadings—his secular government
also gave women more rights than their counterparts in
many other Islamic countries."*
— **Mike Taibbi,** NBC Nightly News, April 22, 2003

*"My daughter, who goes to Stuyvesant High School only blocks
from the World Trade Center, thinks we should fly an American
flag out our window. Definitely not, I say: The flag stands
for jingoism and vengeance and war."*
— **Katha Pollitt,** The Nation, October 8, 2001

You've heard it before: The United States, acting as a tool
of the multinational companies that really control it, has
become an imperial power in the modern world. Through

our powerful military and economic might, we've colonized the planet, even if we don't have the effrontery to actually call this the age of the American Empire. The control the U.S. enjoys is more cunning and subtle than that used in earlier empires, but mystified oppression is still oppression.

Meanwhile, nations in emerging markets are being strip-mined of their raw materials, while their labor forces work at slave wages for the benefit of American corporations. Adding insult to injury, in developed and developing countries alike, America's ersatz and vulgar popular culture spreads everywhere like processed cheese. From Singapore to the Champs-Elysee, rap videos, McDonald's hamburgers, and *Survivor* reruns have taken root, crowding out and finally suffocating the indigenous cultures of native peoples. High culture is being dissolved in the universal solvent of American bad taste, as low culture turns the world into Planet Hollywood.

In this chapter, we'll explore the truth of these charges.

The Military Domination of the United States

In the years leading up to 1940, the United States was isolationist in its foreign policy . . . until we were savagely attacked at Pearl Harbor and in the Philippines and throughout the Pacific. And how did the Japanese treat our prisoners of war (POWs) who surrendered? Ignoring the Geneva convention, they subjected them to sadistic torture too gruesome to describe here. The U.S., forced to enter the war, helped deliver a knockout punch to Nazi Germany and then defeated Japan, releasing the world from these demonic regimes. Then, having expended the lives of more than 400,000 of its young men, with more than a million casualties, and at a total cost of over two trillion of today's dollars, how did America treat these nations?

Unlike previous victors, we seized no meaningful territory permanently and took no spoils, nor did we rape or pillage those we had vanquished. Instead, we instituted something revolutionary: the Marshall Plan, which helped recreate the economic superstructure of Europe. We gave Europe some 80 to 100 billion in today's dollars, an amount that swells to $400 billion if measured as the equivalent percentage of today's gross domestic product. When George Marshall won the Nobel Peace Prize for his plan in 1953, he accepted it on behalf of all Americans, who had shown magnanimity on a scale without historical precedent.

After more than 200,000 POWs had been killed by Japanese atrocities, we responded by providing humanitarian aid to Japan and assisted with rebuilding their country. Emperor Hirohito was even allowed to remain in power, although we made him publicly renounce his "divinity." Before leaving, we installed a constitutional system of government in Japan.

The result: a swift recovery, and a strong and vibrant Germany and Japan, both leading economic powers in the world today.

Next, the U.S. fought and won the Cold War, a 45-year battle to save the world from Communist totalitarianism. This included some 33,000 Americans killed in Korea (at a cost of $264 billion) and more than 47,000 killed in Vietnam (at a cost of some $347 billion). Additionally, the United States was forced to devote trillions of dollars to national defense over this period. Those film clips from the 1950s that show U.S. schoolchildren preparing for nuclear attack by hiding under their desks, the ones that seem so funny now? They weren't so funny back then. The Soviet Union was devoting fully half of its GDP to nuclear weapons and its armed services.

The centrally planned Soviet economy, charged with setting and maintaining some 24 million prices, finally collapsed under its own weight in 1990—unable to compete with the providential Reagan arms buildup. This left only China and Cuba as Communist countries, and even they seem to have abandoned their expansionist ambitions.

These were no small victories. Drawing from Matthew White's *Historical Atlas of the Twentieth Century,* the following table reviews some basic math about the people we fought:

Table 2.1: Death Toll from Despotic Regimes

Cause	Median Estimated Deaths
Lenin & Russian Revolution	8,750,000
Stalin (1924–1953	20,000,000
Hitler (including Holocaust)	35,000,000
Japan—WWII	15,500,000
Communist Revolution—China	6,200,000
Mao Zedong (1949–1975)	45,000,000

In all, a midrange estimate of 120 million people were killed during the past century, and they died under brutal conditions due to the ideas and actions of a few evil but extremely powerful men. The United States took these regimes on, at great cost to itself, and stopped them.

In early 2003, when Episcopalian General Colin Powell was sanctimoniously questioned by a former archbishop of Canterbury about the role of the U.S. military, Powell replied: "We have gone forth from our shores repeatedly over the last hundred years, and we've done this as recently as the last year in Afghanistan. [We've] put wonderful young men and women at risk, many of whom have lost their lives, and we have asked for nothing except enough ground to bury them in . . . otherwise, we have returned home to live our own lives in peace." If the United States has come to be the world's dominant military power, it's a good thing, considering the alternatives. Never has a military with such might been used with such forbearance.

Of course there have been notable failures and glaring omissions along the way, a fact that brings no end of delight to many America-hating liberals. However, had Nazism triumphed throughout Europe and Russia, had Japan been allowed to keep its Asian "co-prosperity sphere," had Communism overrun Southeast Asia and South and Central America, the staggering, unthinkable numbers tabulated on page 33 would be far higher. If these murderers had been given their way, the world would be in chains.

★ ★ ★

One often hears rumors about the U.S. having propped up this or that oppressive dictator around the world; as citizens, we scratch our heads and wonder, *What were they thinking? How could we support such obviously corrupt regimes that are antithetical to our principles? No wonder the people over there hate us.*

However, these sentiments overlook the central tenet of foreign policy, which is the "lesser of two evils" choice. We deal with the world as it is given to us. During the Cold War, for example, it was often necessary to support corrupt rulers around the world to forestall the installation of worse: Communists. Communism spread like a virus across the postwar world, and it led to unprecedented misery for the countries where it took hold. Each of these countries in turn created new staging grounds for assaults upon the United States and other liberal democracies. We had to stop it wherever possible, even if that meant temporarily doing business with some tin-pot dictators along the way.

True, Communist China still executes more prisoners in a week than the United States does in a year, but with the seeds of capitalism planted, it's unlikely to return to its former ways.

China has the atomic bomb, but little incentive to drop it on the U.S., since not only would such an action destroy China's best customer, but it would also possibly lead to a default on the hundreds of billions of dollars' worth of U.S. Treasury securities that country holds. Today, the threat to human freedom comes from Islamic fundamentalism, not Communism (but that's a separate subject). Thanks to the United States, the world has survived to face this challenge. Moreover, the world has survived in a state of unprecedented prosperity and freedom.

Even the current war against terrorism is only anti-Islamic to the extent that terrorists are using Muslim extremism as a pretense to justify the murders they perpetrate. The most striking feature of this war is the consideration with which the U.S. is fighting it: avoiding civilian targets, quick to supply medicine and humanitarian aid, risking our lives in Afghanistan and Iraq to build an infrastructure and leave the countries a far better place than we found them. One only hopes that America has the will to fight this war to its rightful conclusion, and leave a structure of peace to an undeserving world.

The Economic Domination of the United States

You only need turn on the news to see the protests every time the World Trade Organization holds a meeting. The demonstrators believe that, under free-market, capitalist economics, multinational corporations are pulling the puppet strings of the country and putting the planet into a sausage grinder, chewing up workers, natural resources, and the environment in their insatiable lust for money. According to the AFL-CIO union Website, deregulation, privatization, and trade liberalization have conspired to produce terrible results like these:

- Each day, some 250 million children around the world go to work rather than to school.

- Tens of thousands of people are enslaved in forced labor.

- "Free trade" has laid vulnerable ecosystems in the hands of those hungry for cheap natural resources.

In the last chapter, we saw how much the quality of life has improved in America over the past half century—but were these ill-gotten gains? Have Americans and their capitalist cronies elsewhere merely enriched themselves at the expense of the rest of the world?

Let's look at the facts.

Poverty

In the last 40 years, the average income of the earth's citizens has doubled (after inflation). The poorest quintile of the population had an annual income that rose from $551 in 1965 to $1,137 in 1998. According to the United Nations Development Program, world poverty has fallen more during the past 50 years than in the preceding 500. The United Nations report concludes: "The great success in reducing poverty in the 20th century shows that eradicating severe poverty in the first decades of the 21st century is feasible."

That's saying a mouthful. How could the elimination of severe poverty from the world suddenly be within sight? Well, keep in mind that standards for severe poverty around the world are far more stringent than those of the "poverty rate" in the U.S. that we discussed earlier. And consider the following:

During the 19th century, as much as 85 percent of the world's population subsisted on an income of less than one dollar per day; by 1950, this percentage had shrunk to 50 percent. Today, it's roughly 23 percent, in spite of the world's population having more than doubled over the same period. And by 2015, it's projected to fall to 13 percent, according to the *Global Economic Prospects 2003* report from the World Bank. Indian economist Surjit Bhalla, formerly of the World Bank, believes that even these figures overstate the current extent of global poverty: By his calculations, the poverty rate has already fallen to 13 percent.

Why has severe poverty declined so dramatically around the world? The answer is simple: Capitalism plus globalization equals prosperity. Living in a land of unbelievable affluence, it's difficult for Americans to realize that the condition of humanity has always been one of extreme indigence. The near-miraculous shrinkage of poverty from the globe isn't an arbitrary event; it's due to the wealth-creating properties of industrialization and technology, which leverage human capital when organized by free markets under capitalism.

This didn't happen under the top-down, control-and-command, centrally planned economies of Communist countries, despite the cover story they floated about creating a worker's paradise. (Note: When party leaders say they need to provisionally enslave you so that they can ultimately free you, play special attention to the "enslave" part.) After the USSR fell in 1990, Westerners were surprised to learn that this superpower was really a third-world country in terms of living standards. For instance, half the hospitals in Moscow—its most advanced city—had no sewerage, and 80 percent of them lacked hot water.

Hunger

One of the cruelest ways that poverty manifests itself is through hunger. As poverty has fallen, so have stomachs been filled. According to the Food and Agriculture Organization of the United Nations, in 1970 there were 960 million undernourished people in the developing countries—nearly 37 percent of their populations. By 1996, that figure had shrunk to 790 million—less than 18 percent—and it's projected to decline to 12 percent by the year 2010. This is a still a staggering number, but it shouldn't blind us from the dramatic improvement that has been made.

The strides in feeding the hungry have been the greatest in East and Southeast Asia, where hunger has declined 70 percent, followed by North Africa and the Middle East (down 64 percent), Latin America (down 42 percent), and South Asia (down 39 percent). The terrible omission is sub-Saharan Africa, where the decline is a scant 3 percent, and the number of people suffering from hunger has actually increased. It's sadly the case that sub-Saharan Africa is the least touched by globalization of any of these regions.

Thanks to the green revolution, global food production has doubled over the past 50 years, and prices of basic grains like wheat and rice have fallen 60 percent. Pure water, available to only 10 percent of the world's rural population 20 years ago, is now available to 75 percent.

This feeding of the multitudes has come about, not through United Nations CARE packages and church-sponsored soup kitchens, but (among other reasons) because scientists at companies like Monsanto and Novartis have created new strains of crops that are more productive, hardier, and more disease resistant. Newer and more efficient varieties of wheat now account for three-quarters of its production in developing countries.

Since the 1980s, food prices have dropped 50 percent, while the productivity per acre has risen 25 percent—a process that has put billions of dollars into the pockets of the world's poorest farmers and their surrounding villages. In the context of alleviating world hunger, the concerns about bioengineered food held by Europeans and the high-consciousness citizens of Mendocino County, California, seem precious indeed.

Education

Just as a college degree serves as a ticket to the good life in economically developed countries, simple literacy gets people on the ladder to self-improvement everywhere. The most basic form of capital is *human* capital. When human beings invest in themselves by learning to read and write and perform basic computational arithmetic, their lifetime earnings can increase exponentially. Education and economic productivity operate in a mutually reinforcing spiral in developing countries. While there are an estimated 900 million illiterate adults in the world today, this represents 25 to 30 percent of the population in developing countries, a decrease from about 70 percent a half century ago.

Elementary education is now available throughout the world, with the notable exception again being sub-Saharan Africa (although even there it's available to 75 percent of the population). Globally, education is a feminist issue, since 65 percent of those who remain illiterate are girls. Just as education leads to increased prosperity, a certain baseline level of income is required for families to be able to afford to send their daughters to school. This is why globalization is the best hope for the emancipation of women.

Rich vs. Poor

Critics of globalization argue that it has enriched developed nations more than the emerging ones. However, this argument parallels the one we've just considered within the United States: The unfairness of the rich getting richer faster than the poor have increased their earnings, leaving the rich with a bigger piece of the pie. One statistic often repeated is that 20 percent of the earth's population consumes 80 percent of the world's goods and services (sometimes mistranslated as 80 percent of the "earth's resources"). Can this be fair?

In fact, there is no cause-and-effect relationship at work: The rich are not rich at the *expense* of the poor. As the rich have gotten richer, so have the poor. Wealthy nations have grown far wealthier since the end of colonialism than they became while colonialism was still in place. (The United States is itself a former exploited colony.) The reason that 20 percent of the earth's population consumes 80 percent of all goods and services is because it *produces* 80 percent of all goods and services. Unfortunately, the 80 percent that consumes only 20 percent of all goods and services also produces only 20 percent of all goods and services. This is what needs correcting. As Johan Norberg points out in *In Defense of Global Capitalism,* "The uneven distribution of wealth in the world is due to the uneven distribution of capitalism." Or, as expressed by U.N. Secretary-General Kofi Annan, "The main losers in today's very unequal world are not those who are too much exposed to globalization—they are those who have been left out."

Obviously, the world has always been unequal. But Columbia University economist Xavier Sala-i-Martin found that global inequality at the end of 2000 was at its lowest point since World War II. Economists have developed a scale called the "Gini coefficient" to measure inequality. The scale ranges from 0 to 1, with 0 reflecting complete equality between everyone, and 1 representing total inequality (one person owning everything while everyone else owns nothing). For the world as a whole, the Gini coefficient declined from 0.60 in 1968 to 0.52 in 1997, while in the far more egalitarian United States, it fell to 0.41. The relative standard of living for the world's poor has been rising and inequality declining, thanks to globalization.

According to a Fraser Institute report edited by James Gwartney and Robert Lawson, the countries with the greatest degree of economic freedom have the lion's share of economic prosperity. This is because open markets lead to economic development. Prior to the Industrial Revolution, the entire world lived in a state of poverty comparable to that existing only in the very poorest countries today—in fact, Europeans were only about 20 percent better off than the benighted heathen elsewhere. After the Industrial Revolution, the same new technologies were in principle available everywhere, but they didn't flourish equally in all places. Countries inherently rich in natural resources began to lag behind others that simply created better conditions for trade and business, as these in turn grew vastly richer.

The benefit of globalization isn't so everyone can watch MTV and NASCAR, although that may be a by-product. Global capitalism is the Archimedes lever by which economist Adam Smith's "invisible hand" of God is lifting the world out of poverty. This machine isn't hoarded by the "haves"; instead, it can be used by any society that wishes to employ it. Contrary to the complaints of liberal critics, it doesn't happen by a "trickle-down" mechanism, as crumbs spill down from the table of the rich to be fought over by the beggars below. Rather, societies enrich themselves through greater productivity everywhere at once. Even in sub-Saharan Africa, which has been largely shut out of this banquet, the intractable barriers to widespread socioeconomic improvement are primarily political.

Just as there's no mystery about how one climbs out of poverty in America, we know the preconditions for countries to pull themselves out of indigence on a global scale. Every year the Heritage Foundation ranks the nations of the world along its index of economic freedom. Countries that rank high (such as Hong Kong, Ireland, the United States, and Canada) are invariably more prosperous than those that are economically repressed (such as North Korea, Cuba, Iran, and Zimbabwe). The index looks at ten factors that are correlated with economic development:

- The defense of *property rights* is considered an indispensable partner of foreign investment (1).

- Countries that have *open trade policies* can participate in the global market (2).

- Countries that have *low tax burdens* encourage individual initiative (3).

- Economies that have *low government participation* do not crowd out private investment with government-sponsored enterprises (4).

- Business thrives where there is a *light regulatory burden* imposed by government (5) and *market forces set wages and prices* (6).

- Countries with a *stable monetary policy* are likely to attract outside investors (7), as will those that allow the *free flow of capital* in and out of their borders (8).

- Countries with *active banking systems and financial markets* are easy places to do business (9).

- Finally, countries that have *informal markets,* where buyers can get what they need, are more likely to promote growth than societies where certain goods may be scarce at any price (10).

Not every country needs to be a paragon of economic freedom along all ten dimensions in order to prosper, but in general, the more economic freedom, the more prosperity will follow. It may not be in the personal best interest of dictator Kim Jong Il of North Korea to bestow these kinds of reforms upon his impoverished land, but there can be little doubt that, were he to do so, the economic condition of the average North Korean would improve immensely over the coming decade. (South Korea, where such freedoms do exist, is a center of prosperity in Asia.)

Global financial markets exert a salutary discipline on governments that wish to participate in the international marketplace. A country can no longer conduct its economic affairs as it wishes and not face the consequences, as there is no Soviet Union to keep it propped up when its policies falter. If the economy is unstable, inflation looms, or default threatens, the bond market will punish a country by withholding needed funds except at a high rate of interest, as bond vigilantes pull their money out with the click of a mouse. The resulting high cost of capital will make it difficult for the country to compete effectively in the global marketplace. But if markets are stable and orderly, inflation is low, the courts uphold property rights, and there is a strong central bank, then capital will flow in and interest rates will be low.

Exploited Workers

What about all those workers who are supposedly being taken advantage of? We have to remember that people in third-world nations don't work for a few dollars a day because someone is holding a gun to their heads—they do so because they're earning more than they get by working for the village landlord. The alternative to the shoe factory may be no job at all. While these people are poor by American standards, they're much better off than they were before the new factory came to town. And wages can't be high, because productivity isn't high. If, out of an absurd snobbery, we tell poor countries that we won't trade with them until they have a standard of living like our own, they'll never develop their standard of living to a level that we find aesthetically pleasing. For the people involved, the dynamic is a self-improving one. Having gained skills in one setting, these can be transferred elsewhere. As more companies come to the country in search of cheap labor, they must compete for the workers' labor by offering higher wages. As the local labor force becomes more productive, they can be paid more.

Children are often held up as casualties of globalization, but in fact they are its principal beneficiaries. Children in third-world countries are now far more likely to be literate than their parents; while those who work in export industries making clothing, for example, have much better working conditions than those not fortunate enough to have this employment. While Westerners understandably want to help such children, these efforts can and do backfire. According to UNICEF, when the garment industry in Bangladesh in 1993 was pressured by foreigners to release about 50,000 child laborers (primarily girls) from its employ, most found work in far more dangerous activities such as stone crushing, street hustling, and prostitution.

Special-interest groups (like the AFL-CIO we quoted earlier), seeking to be protected or exempted by our government, invariably point to the failures of global capitalization, of which there are no doubt many. But a particular factory closing, or a village where children are still working instead of going to school, shouldn't blind us to the larger picture: Globalization isn't the best thing since sliced bread—it *is* bread itself for billions.

At What Cost?

Even granting that globalization might be a good thing for everyone else outside the industrialized world, what is it costing us? Wouldn't we be better off shutting our borders and leading the good life, with high-paying jobs for all inside our cozy cocoon, while we let the rest of the world play catch-up?

It wouldn't work. The reason why was first divined by economists Adam Smith and David Ricardo in the 18th and 19th centuries: Countries, like individuals, do best when they specialize in producing those goods and services where they have a *comparative advantage*—that is, by selling whatever they do best, and using the proceeds to buy everything else they need. In much of the world, until fairly recently, every family grew or caught its own food, made its own clothes, churned its own butter, and dipped its own candlesticks. Life was hard, and conditions were desperately insecure—dependent on the weather as much as anything, and heaven help you if your cow got sick. As was said in Thomas Hobbes's *Leviathan*, life was ". . . solitary, poor, nasty, brutish, and short." But role specialization meant that some people could farm, if that was what they did best, while others baked bread and still others made clothes. The net result was that life improved for all.

45

Ricardo's proof involved Portuguese wine and English wheat. He demonstrated that, although both wine and wheat could be produced more cheaply in Portugal, the Portuguese and English would both be better off (that is, able to consume more wine and wheat) if each country specialized in the field where it had the greatest comparative advantage—the Portuguese in making wine, the English in growing wheat—than if both countries tried to make both products. With each country doing what it does best, more wine and wheat is produced overall, resulting in more loaves of bread and jugs of wine for each for the same amount of labor.

This is why trade barriers actually serve to lower the standard of living for the citizens within a country that imposes them. If we prohibit or tax the import of strawberries from Chile, we pay more for our own domestic berries. This benefits a few farmers here at home at the expense of all strawberry eaters. Furthermore, it distorts the economy: If berries can be grown more cheaply elsewhere, then providing artificial employment for our outmoded strawberry farmers hinders the economy from adapting to the new global reality of cheaper strawberries for everyone.

The global marketplace is telling our farmers that instead of engaging in expensive, less productive work, they should learn new, more useful skills that will add value to society, not subtract from it. This dislocation may be painful, but the alternative—a drain on society in a way that serves no purpose (except maintaining the domestic strawberry grower's income) is even worse. A trade barrier simply keeps the strawberry farmer from getting the message, at our expense. Progress marches on, and it's no respecter of individual special interests.

Here's another example: If the Chinese government wants to subsidize the production of steel, which it can then "dump" in American markets (since obsolete American steel manufacturers can't compete, although some up-to-date ones can and do), then American consumers benefit, since Chinese citizens are, in effect, paying for a portion of the price of our steel. This is a nice deal for us, and a bad deal for them, so let them "dump" away. If a store is selling DVDs for below its cost, is this a reason for us to stay away? No, the prudent consumer takes the opportunity to stock up.

This doesn't work to our advantage, however, when our own government gets into the act. For example, the U.S. government subsidizes farm products. This is a bad deal for us, but it's beneficial for consumers in other countries. Yet this policy is especially harmful to developing countries, where farming is often an entry-level occupation in an economy that we're snuffing out before it can take hold. In *Adventure Capitalist*, noted investor Jim Rogers describes the lush fields lying fallow outside Lalibela, Ethiopia. Africa actually used to export grain, but today its farmers are unemployed because they can't compete with free grain being handed out at home, or with subsidized Western agriculture abroad.

If we closed the borders and bought only from one another inside the U.S., robbing us of the comparative advantages available from foreign markets, we'd pay higher prices for the same goods and therefore have a lower quality of life. Some interest groups (car manufacturers, for example) might benefit, but as consumers, we'd pay the price for this decreased competition. Of course, it's easy to point to car workers laid off from a U.S. plant, but harder to show that the higher price of cars paid by the rest of us is the price for keeping them happily underemployed at the factory, and that this cost to the rest of us takes its own toll.

The logic of protectionism extends still further: Why should Floridians buy from Massachusetts? Why should Miamians buy from Tampa? Why should people who live in South Beach buy from the mainland? This way of thinking quickly devolves into every family out for themselves, living on a self-sufficient farm, but at the lowest standard of living. This is precisely the predicament that free trade rescued us from in the first place, by allowing every country to express its comparative advantage in the open market. When times get tough, the howls for protectionism grow the loudest. Conveniently forgotten is the Smoot-Hawley Tariff of 1930 (see *Ferris Bueller's Day Off* for a stimulating lecture on this tariff by one of your authors), which helped take the stock market crash—and the U.S. economic slowdown—and export it into a worldwide depression.

Remember Ross Perot's warning of "a giant sucking sound" when NAFTA went into effect a decade ago, as American jobs swooshed to Mexico? It never happened. Instead, the number of jobs in the U.S. increased by millions, and our unemployment rate fell to its lowest level in years. According to the Office of the U.S. Trade Representative, NAFTA and the Uruguay Round together "generate annual benefits of $1,300–$2,000 annually for the average American family of four."

The Cultural Imperialism of the United States

Even if the export of capitalism, democracy, and industrialization is saving the world, there are still the effects of U.S. culture to consider:

"The concept of cultural imperialism today best describes the sum of the process by which society is brought into the modern world system and how its dominating stratum is attracted, pressured, forced, and sometimes bribed into shaping social institutions to correspond to, or even promote, the values and structures of the dominating center of the system. . . . The content and style of

programming, however adapted to local conditions, bear the ideo-logical imprint of the main centers of the capitalist world economy."
— **Herbert I. Schiller,** Communication and Cultural Domination

"[T]he onrush of economic and ecological forces . . . demand integration and uniformity and that mesmerize the world with fast music, fast computers, and fast food—with MTV, Macin-tosh, and McDonald's, pressing nations into one commercially homogeneous global network: one McWorld tied together by technology, ecology, communications, and commerce."
— **Benjamin R. Barber,** Jihad vs. McWorld

This contretemps is nothing new. As far back as 1901, British writer William Stead's *The Americanization of the World* warned that America was steamrollering over the multiple languages, tra-ditions, and identities of cultures around the world. So what about those *Temptation Island* episodes and Britney Spears CDs that are all over Europe and Asia? Or the Bee Gees' (although, strictly speaking, they were an Australian group) music playing in the discos of the Middle East? Is this bad? Should we be wor-ried about U.S. cultural hegemony?

The simple truth is, no one is "making" the world consume U.S. popular culture. People do so because they choose to. If peo-ple want to wear sunglasses like Keanu Reeves, is this really a prob-lem? It may not be entirely to our taste, but who are we to pre-vent anyone else from spending their dollars or pesos or yen in the way they wish? After all, the French banned the sale of that decadent Yankee drink Coca-Cola after World War II, but they finally relented in 1953, and the *Tour d'Eiffel* is still standing.

Since the U.S. has been taking in refugees from around the world for hundreds of years, it's famously a cultural melting pot. Our taste in popular entertainment is universally appreciated because it's the road-tested product of a polymorphous culture.

If a movie, TV show, or CD sells in America, it already appeals to a tremendously wide range of tastes. A French film will appeal primarily to the French; an Indian film, primarily to Indians—but American films appeal to everyone. In most cases, our offerings are vastly superior to the inexpensive, grainy, low-production-value pop-culture offerings available abroad (much of which is violent and oppressive to women). Compared to soap operas in third-world countries, *The Young and the Restless* looks like Shakespeare. And who says you can't have both (or all three)?

Some American tourists are troubled when, having gone to all the trouble and expense of taking a vacation abroad, they find vestiges of American life like McDonald's across the street from their hotels. But consider this from the point of view of the citizen of Tokyo, Paris, or Rome: They don't want to live in a city under glass, a foreign Colonial Williamsburg. Just as we appreciate having Japanese, French, and Italian restaurants in our cities, they want American fast food in theirs. For the "pure" foreign experience—Dutch people in wooden shoes, Mexicans in sombreros—one only need go to Epcot at Walt Disney World. (Later, we'll see that this nostalgic yearning for the fatherland, a place of perfection that used to be, is also an animating force behind the environmental movement.)

In no land has there been more reverence for diversity than in the United States of America today. Diversity is the new national religion, the value by which all others are transvalued, the unmediated good in itself. This is why, even as the world has developed an insatiable appetite for American popular culture, U.S. tourists continue their quest for authentic cultural diversity, lavishing their dollars upon it wherever it can be found, from the towers of San Gimignano to the rain forests of Costa Rica. In fact, the continued existence of some indigenous cultures is deeply dependent on the money spent by U.S. travelers and consumers.

There may be an American pop-culture empire for the moment, but it's held together with strands of gossamer. It can be expected to lose ground precisely as offerings from other cultures become more competitive, which they undoubtedly will. The entire planet will be enriched as a result of competition in the arts, just as it has been by competition in the marketplace.

★★★ ★★★

Racism

"After years of enduring America at home and watching her abroad, I am convinced that I will die in a society as racially divided as the one into which I was born more than a half century ago."
— **Randall Robinson,** commentator, 1998

"Racism is an integral, permanent, and indestructible component of this society."
— **Derrick Bell,** Ivy League professor, 1993

"In white America, cultural conservatism takes the form of a chronic racism, sexism, and homophobia . . . for white America, this means primarily scapegoating black people, women, gay men, and lesbians."
—**Cornel West,** Ivy League professor, 1993

"God will destroy America by the hands of Muslims."
— **Louis Farrakhan,** 1996

"White folks was in caves while we was building empires. . . .
We taught philosophy and astrology and mathematics before
Socrates and them Greek homos ever got around to it."
— **Rev. Al Sharpton,** 1994

W hat does the Left find in America today regarding race relations? They see a racist majority oppressing afflicted minorities. And these minorities aren't merely entitled to legal protection against discrimination, but they also require preferential treatment under the law so that no one group is underrepresented in colleges, employment, or any meaningful field of endeavor.

Why do minorities require special handling? Since, as every good liberal knows, all people are the same, any inequality of outcome can only be due to inequality of opportunity. If we can't point to any overt discrimination that's holding minorities back, then this is merely because racism has become institutionalized and invisibly woven into the very fabric of our society. Minorities today are being held back by wires too thin to see. But even though racism is insidiously invisible, liberals claim that its effects are evident, and that's what we'll look at in this chapter.

A Brief History of Racism

Throughout history, human beings have perceived those as "different" to be a threat. When unfamiliar persons came a-calling, they were as likely to burn our fields and rape and murder us as they were to wish us a nice day. Over the millennia, this has ingrained in us humans a certain wariness toward the "other" that prevents the world from being like an advertisement for the United Colors of Benetton. These suspicions have added considerable survival value over time, even if by today's precious standards they've made us all too inclined to throw a rock first and ask questions later.

Ages ago, there may have been a group of Homo sapiens who sang "We Are the World" in perfect harmony and greeted all men and women as their brothers and sisters, but they didn't survive to pass their genes down to those of us living today. Probably, they were eaten. Although we think of primitive man as living in some utopian theme park of the kind swooned over by Rousseau and anthropologist Margaret Mead, the reality was decidedly otherwise: Evidence points to murder as one of the leading causes of death in early human society.

Racism is often conflated with the problem of slavery because of their coincidence in the United States. However, slavery is an equal opportunity employer. One can be a slaveholder without being prejudiced in the least. The ancient Romans who kept Greek slaves nonetheless held Greek culture in the highest esteem. Slavery is essentially an *economic* institution, yet racialist theories were a convenient way to overcome any cognitive dissonance that may have arisen from moral qualms about owning another human being in 19th-century America. These were qualms that the possibly less sensitive Romans, for example, may never have felt.

The word *slave* actually comes from *Slav*. The Slavs were held as slaves far longer than the blacks in America were; most notoriously by the Islamic Turks. However, it was the Arab nations that principally excelled in black slavery, taking in more slaves than did the entire Western Hemisphere. In addition, the mortality rate of slaves going across the Sahara desert was even greater than that of those who made the grim Atlantic passage. (The United States wasn't even the leader in the Western Hemisphere; that unenviable title goes to Brazil, who took in six times as many slaves as we did.)

What happened to all the black slaves in the Middle East? Although America now has tens of millions of citizens whose ancestors were slaves, today you can travel from one end of the Arab world to the other and not meet an indigenous black person. It's enough to make one wonder about the eventual fate of all their human chattel.

The black Africans who became enslaved were predominantly done so by other black Africans; they were then sold to Arab slave traders who, in turn, sold them to European slave traders. It's a sad fact of human history that people enslave other people, a phenomenon that transcends any one race. Africans, Arabs, Asians, American Indians, Hebrews, Christians, and more have all done it. This scarcely excuses the practice, but it does show how widespread it has been.

Unfair though it may be to impose our moral standards on previous historical epochs, the dismal truth is that everybody, everywhere, has blood on his or her ancestral hands when it comes to slavery. As Orlando Patterson writes in *Slavery and Social Death:* "Slavery has existed from the dawn of human history right down to the 20th century, in the most primitive societies and in the most civilized. . . . Probably there is no group of people whose ancestors were not at one time slaves or slaveholders."

In the United States, the framers thought that the issue of slavery was too big and too controversial to be solved at the same time the new Constitution was being hammered out, so they passed the buck to future generations. The notorious clause in the Constitution that assigns representation on the basis of counting "three-fifths" of the non-free population of a state is often stretched to argue that our country's founders thought that slaves were only three-fifths human. Actually, this was a political maneuver by anti-slavery forces to keep the pro-slavery South from gaining too much representation in the new government.

Then again, some of the founding fathers wrongly believed that the institution of slavery was in economic decline, doomed in any event to collapse under its own weight within a short time. (Saint Paul had made a similar mistake in the first century, believing that, with the end of the world imminent, there was little need for a slave or anyone else to worry about his social position.) Others, like Thomas Jefferson, who were themselves slave owners, didn't intellectually believe in the heinous practice in which they were nevertheless implicated. It's human nature to continually fall short—even very short—of one's ideals. Fallible human beings cheat on their taxes, rob banks, have abortions, commit murder, and do all manner of things great and small that in their better moments they might wish they hadn't done. The corruption of slavery present at the founding of the United States can't be overlooked or denied, but neither does it by itself repudiate everything the country stands for.

The key fact about slavery in the United States is that, for the first time, men of the race that enslaved another race fought to free that enslaved race, even giving up their lives in huge numbers to do so. This heroism and nobility was without parallel in human history. It must also be pointed out, because it's often overlooked, that this battle was joined by 180,000 blacks who fought alongside the whites, risking their lives in the Union army, with deeply impressive courage and skill. It took the Civil War to end slavery in the U.S., and more than half a million men died in that war (one for every six slaves freed). We can't be grateful enough for their sacrifices, of which we are the direct moral beneficiaries. This is worth reflecting upon at a juncture when our own country is once again being summoned to make sacrifices for the benefit of future generations. Britain did not do it. France did not do it. Russia did not do it. Only the U.S. did it.

The condition of blacks in America after 1865 was abysmal—their oppression during Reconstruction and up until the 1960s was despicable and humiliating for a nation founded on the concept of "equality." Yet their subsequent struggle for dignity created the third American Revolution. (The first was the Revolutionary War and the battle for independence; the second was the Civil War and the end of slavery; and the third was the battle for civil rights, the war against racism and discrimination.) The story of that movement is a glorious chapter in the history of America.

The Battle for Civil Rights

To set the record straight, despite the dismissive portrayal of the 1950s as years of mindless conformity, they were in many ways the apogee of American civilization. The era that spanned Miles Davis's *Birth of the Cool* in 1948 and ended with the Kennedy assassination and the Beatles in 1963 gave us modern jazz and rock 'n' roll. It gave us Kerouac, Ginsberg, *The Catcher in the Rye, Lolita, The Caine Mutiny,* and *The Old Man and the Sea.* It gave us the sitcom, *The Tonight Show, MAD Magazine, My Fair Lady, South Pacific,* and *Cat on a Hot Tin Roof.* It gave us the Corvette and the Kinsey reports. It gave us the Salk polio vaccine, the pacemaker, and the structure of DNA.

This was the decade when the Pulitzer prize for poetry went to the likes of Carl Sandburg and Wallace Stevens; while the Nobel Prize for literature went to William Faulkner, Ernest Hemingway, Albert Camus, Bertrand Russell, Winston Churchill, and John Steinbeck. And just take a look at a list of the films (*Sunset Boulevard, Father of the Bride, The African Queen, High Noon, From Here to Eternity, Roman Holiday, On the Waterfront, Marty, The Bridge on the River Kwai, 12 Angry Men,* and *The Apartment*) and actors (Spencer Tracy, James Stewart, Humphrey Bogart, Marlon Brando, Alec Guinness, Gary Cooper, Audrey Hepburn, Burt Lancaster, Richard Burton, James Dean, Katharine Hepburn, Jack Lemmon, Kirk Douglas, Ingrid Bergman, Lana Turner, Elizabeth Taylor, Paul Newman, Deborah Kerr, and Laurence Olivier) who received Academy Award nominations in the 1950s and you will faint. Nevertheless, as flat-out sensational as times were in the '50s, there was a gigantic worm in the apple: racism—a cruel and humiliating national epidemic.

One of your authors lived in a pleasant neighborhood in suburban Maryland about a mile from a black (or as we said then, "colored") neighborhood. Whites had green lawns and swimming pools; blacks had no indoor plumbing, trash in front of their homes, and often lacked electricity—and they were routinely called horrible names. In fact, the author's sixth-grade teacher endlessly told the class his favorite joke: "What do you call a colored necktie salesman?" Answer: "A tycoon." This was from a teacher in a public school!

The struggle to end discrimination was far more difficult than we remember today. Racism used to be basic in American life, and segregation was common practice. Signs in restaurants said: WHITE TRADE ONLY. Ads for apartments read: "Near to churches" (translation: No Jews). Even in *The Washington Post*, that bastion of liberalism, classified ads for jobs and dwellings were broken down by "White" and "Colored." This sort of thing had gone on for a hundred years, and it seemed as if it would go on forever. It was just the way things were.

Discrimination by race was curtailed by several developments. Adolf Hitler had made us aware of the consequences of racism; and the internal tension of America fighting against the world's most racist regime—yet itself being a bigoted country—began to be unbearable. Out of this contradiction came the civil rights movement, led, to be fair, by American liberals. The

Supreme Court ended school segregation and struck down the infamous "separate but equal" doctrine from the 1896 *Plessy v. Ferguson* case in the epic *Brown v. Board of Education* decision in 1954. This, in turn, was followed by dramatic and brave acts to secure civil rights in this country: Sit-ins. Mass arrests. Demonstrations. People getting beaten up, but keeping on with the struggle. In the South, blacks were being killed and their bodies secretly dumped.

Then, in 1964, something so shocking happened that the tide was decisively turned against segregation. Two white, Jewish civil rights workers from the North, Andrew Goodman and Michael Schwerner, were peacefully riding in a car with James Earl Chaney, a black man from Mississippi, when they were stopped by the Ku Klux Klan, itself being led by a local Mississippi deputy sheriff. All three men were brutally murdered and buried in an earthen dam. Suddenly, gone forever was any pretense of legitimacy by the segregationists, and the outrage of the nation led to the passing of the Civil Rights Act of 1964. This act changed everything: housing, transportation, and accommodations; and jobs were suddenly open to everyone by virtue of federal law. (Although it was intended for blacks, the act's implications would soon prove to be equally powerful for Jews and women.) Finally, the Voting Rights Act of 1965 fully restored the franchise to black Americans.

We owe tremendous debts to the men and women who fought for civil rights in the United States, from Rosa Parks to Medgar Evers and, above all, to Dr. Martin Luther King, Jr., who led us on a moral crusade as important as any we fought abroad. This fight transformed the country from a caste society to one based on merit—or, as one might say, from a society based on status to one based on contract, and we all reap the dividends every day (just read the previous two chapters if you don't believe it).

What's vital to remember is that when we see the films of demonstrators marching back then, there are almost always large numbers of white people present along with the blacks. The movement was led by African Americans, of course, but it was enthusiastically joined in by Caucasians. Once again, the oppressor class had joined the oppressed in huge numbers to fight for its freedom. Try to imagine this in another country. Try to imagine, for example, the German Jews demonstrating against the Nuremburg racial laws—with thousands of Aryans walking arm in arm with them. It is a sad exercise in an impossibility.

Then and Now

Jim Heimann's *All American Ads* features a richly colored compendium of print advertisements from the middle decades of the 20th century. Often beautifully drawn or photographed with an imagination and an earnestness we rarely see today, these ads—for automobiles, airplanes, movies, appliances, clothing, travel, and everything else that was for sale or needed promoting—are glorious examples of the power of Madison Avenue. But there's something eerie and unsettling about these ads as well: The men, women, and kids depicted in them look happy, resolute, intelligent, and are often square jawed and determined.

One more thing: They're all white.

Sure, there are a few blacks in white jackets and bow ties, serving drinks on a club car; there's one maid talking silly black dialect and threatening to quit because the refrigerator is too noisy; and there are a few Pullman porters helping a white person with his luggage. But generally speaking, nonwhite people simply didn't exist in the ads of those days. Just as in the movies and TV and radio programs of the time, they appeared mostly as caricatures and/or as servants. A man from Mars would have thought that there were only a few blacks in America in the '40s and '50s, and they only existed to serve whites—with a smile.

What a change we're experiencing in advertising! Ads now feature men, women, and children of every racial background, and nonwhite Americans don't have to feel that Madison Avenue considers them invisible. Today's advertising world, whatever its defects in creative terms, depicts us all. In a way, this is in itself a sign of the triumph of our country's best ideals over the explicit racism we battled against in World War II and the less blatant homegrown bigotry we fought in the '50s and '60s. It's heartening to see how incredibly far we've traveled . . . and that it's been in the right direction.

These images graphically show what the numbers say about the progress of African Americans since the end of segregation. The advertisements are being paid for by corporate America, not out of the goodness of their hearts, but because they now must court minorities due to their purchasing power. And when you have purchasing power, the white man—or any man or woman of any color—pays respect.

And the change in black economic power has been staggering. Consider that in 1940, 2 percent of physicians were black. In 1998, that percentage increased to 5 percent (of a much larger overall population). In 1940, only half of one percent of attorneys were black. In 1998, that figure had increased to 4 percent. In 1940, only one-tenth of one percent of engineers were black. In 1998, it was 4 percent. Blacks are still underrepresented compared to their presence in the general population, but does anyone doubt that this is destined to change over time? Does anyone actually think that there's a professional society or school anywhere in this country that would frown on admitting a person because of his or her race?

In 1940, a black male could expect to earn 44 cents for every dollar his white counterpart earned; in 1998, it was 76 cents. Now, does the remaining gap of 24 cents mean that institutionalized racism is currently oppressing the black man? While at first blush it might look like both men are working side by side on the assembly line, with the white guy taking home a fatter paycheck than his black brother, this isn't actually the case. The white man, on average, is better educated, so he's doing work that pays more (at least for now). In fact, of course, it is illegal to pay people of the same qualifications doing the same work less because of their race or sex or ethnicity.

Moving ahead a few years, the proportion of black families earning more than $75,000 almost tripled between 1970 and 2000, to 13 percent; while the percentage of black households earning more than $50,000 annually jumped 81 percent from 1980 to 2000 (by comparison, the percentage of white households earning more than $50,000 grew only 60 percent over the same period). Stock ownership grew 30 percent among these black households, while it increased only 4 percent among whites with comparable incomes. The number of blacks below the poverty line has fallen from 55 percent in 1959 to 24 percent in 2002. This is still too many, but the progress has been spectacular.

In 1983, 14 percent of blacks worked at professional and managerial jobs; in 2002, that figure had grown to 23 percent. African Americans are well on their way to catching up with whites, of whom 32 percent hold professional or managerial jobs. During the 1982 recession, the layoff rate for blacks was 45 percent greater than for whites; today, they're laid off at the same rate. Meanwhile, the number of black women working as domestic servants has fallen to one percent of employed black females, down from 6 percent in 1983.

Since education is the one-way ticket to progress, it's heartening to note that, while in 1980 only 51 percent of blacks earned their high school diplomas, by 2002 that number had jumped to 79 percent. Similarly, the percentage graduating from college has doubled over this time frame, from 8 to 17 percent. Today, 25 percent of black men go to college, as do 35 percent of black women. Of course, it is debatable what a high school degree means at this point in terms of actually knowing anything, just as it is with a college degree. But there are immense additions to income for owning such degrees, so they must mean something.

The Myth of Institutionalized Racism

As Lee Daniels of the National Urban League concludes, "Black people have made enormous strides since the 1960s, when two-thirds [of them] were poor or working class. Now two-thirds are working class, middle class, and even upper class." Or, as Michael Steele, the lieutenant governor of Maryland, puts it, "This is recognizing the third element of Martin Luther King, Jr.'s, agenda: First was civil rights; second was political representation; and the third, which he did not get a chance to fulfill, was economic empowerment. These mechanisms have been put in place, enabling us to achieve the American Dream."

More than 50 years ago, in 1953, we saw the last full year that racial segregation of the schools in the southern and border states was legal and enforceable under the Constitution. Fifty years ago, a black parent trying to register his son or daughter at the elementary school one of your authors attended could have been criminally sanctioned. Fifty years ago, there were only token numbers of African Americans and almost no Hispanic Americans or Asian Americans in the prestigious schools of the nation.

Fifty years ago, there was one black man in the U.S. Congress, Adam Clayton Powell, Jr., Democrat of Harlem—it would have been a joke for a black man to even be considered as secretary of state, and a black man running for President would have been the setup for racist humor.

In that short span of time, this has all changed dramatically—and without a war or major bloodshed. The last vestiges of public school segregation vanished during the presidency of Richard Nixon, almost 35 years ago. The big-name schools of this nation have richly diverse racial enrollments. Yale Law School had maybe three or four blacks per class when one of your authors entered in the late 1960s—it's now about 20 percent minorities. Today the Congressional Black Caucus has roughly 40 members and is one of the most powerful blocs in the Congress. We have a distinguished man of color as secretary of state, a black woman of great talent as national security advisor, other blacks in the cabinet and sub-cabinet, and a courageous man of color on the Supreme Court. This is astounding progress, although you rarely see it on the news.

The top-ranking scientific graduate schools of the nation are overflowing with other minorities, especially Asians, many of whom came here under appalling circumstances—yet they're now at the head of their classes. You rarely see this as a sign of the openness in our society, but it's news indeed. Fifty years ago, blacks or Asians in top corporate jobs would have been unimaginable. Now, the head of Merrill Lynch, Stanley O'Neal, is a black man—so is Kenneth Chenault, the head of American Express; Richard Parsons, head of Time Warner; and Franklin Raines, head of Fannie Mae. The heads of a plethora of high-tech companies are Asian Americans; and the corporate law firms of Los Angeles, Dallas, and Austin are studded with Hispanic Americans. This is a radically changed nation.

Crime remains a vastly larger problem for blacks and Hispanics than for whites, and so do single-parent families, drug use, and other pathologies. But the statistical and anecdotal data overwhelmingly shows that this is a wide-open society for hardworking, disciplined, and educated men and women of all races. We've achieved a revolution of morality that's unique and that marks a distinct break with history. This onrushing flood of achievement and progress in a free society is what the rest of the world envies, and is why so much of the world wants to come here (even if it's also why some people want to destroy us).

It's still very much morning in America, as Ronald Reagan used to say. America is a great country still in its great days. There's almost no institutional racism, and certainly no official racism left (except for affirmative action, which is explicitly racist—but in some ways understandable). Relations among the races are cordial at almost every level one sees. Yet blacks, who have experienced the most thorough revolution in human advancement in world history over the past 50 years, are told by their would-be leaders that it's as if nothing has been accomplished—they're still living back in the days of the Klan. This is false, divisive, and extremely harmful.

Unfortunately, such rhetoric has been picked up and trumpeted by white left-wingers like Al Gore. All they're doing is inciting paranoia and ensuring that our racial wounds will fester by telling minorities that they can't be expected to succeed without preferential treatment. What better way to breed white resentment, along with black defeatism and a victim mentality? For that matter, if anyone really believed that qualified blacks were being unfairly held back by the system, it would be a simple matter to open a business and hire blacks exclusively, arbitraging their underpaid skills to trounce the competition in the marketplace. But this we don't see—the real point is the shakedown.

As Booker T. Washington noted nearly a century ago, "There is another class of colored people who make a business of keeping the troubles, the wrongs, and the hardships of the Negro race before the public. Having learned that they are able to make a living out of their troubles, they have grown into the settled habit of advertising their wrongs—partly because they want sympathy and partly because it pays. Some of these people do not want the Negro to lose their grievances, because they do not want to lose their jobs."

The war on racism has already been won; however, black leaders and white liberals are trying to snatch defeat from the jaws of victory in order to secure ongoing positions of power and influence for themselves and for the Democratic party. The fact is that today, the doors to achievement are open to every race in America, the freest country on earth in this regard. Unfortunately, there's no political capital to be made by the Left in acknowledging how good things are—their only advantage lies in claiming that the White Citizens' Council and the Republican party are essentially identical. This is an *Alice in Wonderland* inversion of reality. It is also thoroughly cynical.

If Dr. King came back to life today, he'd scarcely be able to believe the progress minorities have made in creating a society in which the content of people's character, not the color of their skin, is decisive in their achievement. This triumph was bought with his blood; to deny it is to deny his achievements and his greatness.

★★★ ★★★

Sexism

"Sexism is a way of life in America's schools."
— **Myra and David Sadker,** *Failing at Fairness:*
How Our Schools Cheat Girls, 1994

"In America, too, successfully persuading women to collaborate in
their own subjugation is a tradition of particularly long standing."
— **Susan Faludi,** *Backlash:*
The Undeclared War Against American Women, 1991

"You study American history now, and what is America
but the history of the enslavement of women. There's no question
but it's become the doctrine."
— **Allan Bloom,** 1987

"For women of ability in America today, I am convinced that there
is something about the housewife state itself that is dangerous."
— **Betty Friedan,** *The Feminine Mystique,* 1963

> *"[H]etereosexuality . . . is a prime cause of*
> *black women's oppression in America."*
> — **Cheryl Clarke,** 1983

> *"When we talk about battery we are not talking*
> *about something that only happens to a few women; we're*
> *talking about something that happens to as many as half the*
> *married women in the United States."*
> — **Andrea Dworkin,** *Life and Death,* 1997

> *"[I]n the United States . . . discrimination remains*
> *strong despite feminist efforts to raise awareness of both*
> *overt and subtle women-hatred."*
> — **Marilyn French,** *The War Against Women,* 1992

I s America a sexist, anti-woman country that is trying to control women's bodies? Does the Right seek to keep women in captivity? In this chapter, we'll look at sexism in the United States.

A Brief History of Feminism

How we relate the history of the women's movement in America depends on our initial assumptions. From the point of view of a women's studies department, we get Marxist dialectic in drag: Starting from Neolithic, matriarchal, goddess-worshiping societies where war and strife were unknown and people lived in ecological balance with nature, men somehow gained the upper hand. Subsequent history is merely the story of wars and gender oppression (males oppressing females), leading to a revolution today as women break free from their shackles to reclaim their power and move toward some indeterminate future "sextopia."

To put it more conventionally, hunting-and-gathering societies, as well as agrarian civilizations, demanded a considerable degree of sex-role specialization, whereby men hunted and labored in the fields while women cooked, sewed, cleaned, and raised children. With the advent of complex modern capitalism, increasing role specialization made many more jobs available, and women were able to move from almost purely domestic responsibilities to earning a living right next to men in the workforce.

Of course, this transition, still in process, didn't occur without a struggle. In 19th-century America and England, married women couldn't easily own property, file for a divorce, or conduct their own affairs. Employers exploited females ruthlessly, and society failed to allow them to earn their real productive worth (although they were paid more than they earned in their agricultural roles). In the 1880s, feminist pioneers such as Elizabeth Cady Stanton, Susan B. Anthony, and Sojourner Truth led the battle for emancipation—a fight to own property, to get an education, to vote, and to work. In 1920, with the Nineteenth Amendment, American women won that right to vote, and a new era opened, witnessed by unchaperoned dating, skirts worn above the knee, makeup, smoking, and dancing—all trivial, to be sure, but also accompanied by great advances in education and women's opportunities. World War II created an acute shortage of labor, which put women into factories earning far more than they'd ever earned before. This opened women's eyes to their new economic power—and it opened employers' eyes to what a precious asset females were in terms of their intelligence and productivity. With this economic power came political power on an immense scale.

Combined with the civil rights movement, the second stage of the women's rights movement followed, this time based on economic and political power as much as on appeals to morality. Laws were passed that made it illegal to pay men and women differently for the same work. In many states, no-fault divorce laws were passed. The Pill and liberalized abortion laws dramatically reduced the chances of unwanted children. As a result, American women are now among the most liberated in the world.

With a valued assist from *Women's Figures,* a book by Diana Furchtgott-Roth and Christine Stolba, let's review some of this progress:

Education

One hundred years ago, even as few as forty years ago, women were barred from entering some of the most prestigious universities. Today, the country's current college freshman class is 55 percent female and 45 percent male. In fact, women now earn most of the nation's bachelor's and master's degrees. In 1970, 13 percent of Ph.D.'s went to women. Today, 41 percent do. Within a decade, women are projected to receive the majority of doctorate degrees as well.

Women earned 4 percent of law degrees in 1956; by 1998, they earned 44 percent. Women earned less than 1 percent of dentistry degrees in 1952; by 1998, they earned 38 percent. Women received 5 percent of the M.D.'s in 1952; by 1998, they took 42 percent. In 2003, 50 percent of first-year medical-school classes were made up of females.

This is astonishing, revolutionary progress. But to the die-hard complainers, it's not enough. The hidden agenda of our educational system is to oppress women, according to gender feminists (who themselves have been given an unprecedented red-carpet reception throughout the elite universities of America). Girls supposedly are ignored by teachers, are fearful of asking for help, and are dominated by boys in the classroom, according to a 1991 report by the American Association of University Women. Yet statistics show that, based on most indicators of academic equity, there are no significant differences between boys and girls. Boys do slightly better at math and science, but overall, girls are the superior students. The writing skills of 8th-grade girls are comparable to those of 11th-grade boys. In fact, in *The War Against Boys,* Christina Hoff Sommers argues that it is young boys who really need remedial education.

Money and Careers

Here are a few more feathers in women's caps:

- Today, according to the Small Business Administration, women own 9.1 million companies, up from 400,000 in the early 1970s—a rise from 5 percent to more than 33 percent of the total.

- The Bureau of Labor Statistics reports that in 1983, 22 percent of women were employed in managerial and professional positions. In 2002, the number had grown to 34 percent.

- A study by executive recruiters Korn/Ferry showed that while in 1973 only 11 percent of corporations had women on their boards of directors, by 1998 that number had grown to 72 percent. And the International Labor Organization reports that American women are represented more often at the highest levels of management than their counterparts in other developed countries, such as Canada, Germany France, England, and Australia.

- Of the 1.5 million Americans who held the job title "Chief Executive" in 2003, 24 percent of them were women, according to the Current Population Survey.

- In 1820, women's average earnings are estimated to have been approximately one-third of men's; by the end of the 19th century, this had risen to 54 percent. By 1980, this figure reached 60 percent; by 1990, it reached 72 percent; and by 1999, women working full-time earned 73 percent of what full-time working men earned.

This last figure is routinely paraded to show how women are still oppressed by men. The problem is, the gap between men's and women's wages doesn't compare what anyone is actually doing to earn the money. For example, if all the men were investment bankers and all the women were housemaids, we wouldn't be surprised to find a still greater disparity—even Marxists don't suggest that everyone should be paid the same.

The "wage gap" is a statistic that conveniently ignores all the factors that actually determine wages: education, training, experience, total hours worked per week, and consecutive years on the job. This last point is key, as women leave the labor force far more often than men (for example, to have children), and therefore accrue less seniority. This is a clear and convincing, although ideologically unexciting, explanation of the difference between what men and women earn. As pointed out by Dr. June O'Neill in the early '70s by a report of the Council of Economic Advisers, it's nonetheless ignored by feminists. But once you control all these factors, the purported wage gap almost disappears—anything remaining probably reflects the price women pay for seeking work that offers the benefit of flexibly shuttling in and out of the workforce.

The principal economic problem of American women today is their greater likelihood of being poor. In 2001, women were more likely to be below the poverty line than men: 12.9 percent to 10.4 percent, respectively. Unfortunately, this problem doesn't lend itself to any simple statutory correction, as most of the women who are poor are either young, unmarried single mothers, or widows who have outlived both their husbands and their savings. Naturally, these are genuine problems that must be addressed, but they're hardly textbook examples of sexism and gender oppression.

Feminists believe that most women have been socialized by a supposedly dominating patriarchal social system into preferring low-paying jobs where they're forever ghettoized and kept uncompetitive with men. Alternately, it may be that even college-educated women (who by now must be exquisitely attuned to all manner of injustice against themselves) choose to make the career compromises dictated by motherhood. If women were really being discriminated against and being paid far less than the true value of their labor, then it would be a simple matter for companies to hire females exclusively and parlay their cheap productivity into higher profits. But this doesn't happen. The true story of women in the American labor force isn't one of exploitation and repression, except in the distant past.

Athletics

President Richard Nixon signed Title IX of the Federal Education Amendments of 1972 into law, banning sex discrimination in schools receiving federal funds. The law is best known for its impact on athletics, as it gave women an equal opportunity to participate in sports in our nation's schools. While this legislation has been extremely controversial, the explosion of women's athletics ever since is undeniable. Before Title IX, there were only 32,000 women on intercollegiate teams; today, there are 150,000. Soccer, the most popular women's college sport, soared from 1,855 participants in 1981–82 to 18,548 in 2000–01, a tenfold increase. Only 3 percent of colleges offered women's soccer in 1977; now 88 percent field women's soccer teams. In 1972, there were only two female athletic teams (of any type) on average per college; by 2000, there were more than eight female teams per school.

The improvement at the high school level is just as dramatic: Before the law, there were 830,000 girls on competitive high school teams; in 2003, there were 2.86 million (according to the National Federation of State High School Associations). In 1972–73, high schools fielded a total of 373 women's softball teams; by 1999–2000, that number climbed to more than 13,000.

Consider some of the following milestones American women have achieved in athletics in recent years:

- 1977: Janet Guthrie becomes the first woman driver in the Indianapolis 500.

- 1984: Joan Benoit Samuelson wins the gold medal in the first Olympic women's marathon.

- 1985: Libby Riddles wins the Iditarod Trail Sled Dog Race—the first woman to do so.

- 1986: Ann Bancroft becomes the first woman to reach the North Pole by dogsled.

- 1987: Jackie Joyner-Kersee is the first female athlete to be featured on the cover of *Sports Illustrated.*

- 1991: The U.S. women's soccer team wins the first FIFA Women's World Cup.

- 1993: Julie Krone wins the Belmont Stakes, riding Colonial Affair to a two and one-quarter length victory.

- 1995: America3, the first all-women's team, competes in the America's Cup race.

- 1996: The U.S. women win gold medals in basketball, gymnastics, soccer, softball, and synchronized swimming at the Olympics in Atlanta.

- 1998: Women's ice hockey makes its Olympic debut in Nagano, with the U.S. team winning the first gold medal.

- 1999: The U.S. women's soccer team wins the FIFA World Cup over China 1–0 in a shoot-out in front of a worldwide television audience of one billion people.

- 2000: Venus Williams became the second African American woman to win Wimbledon. Other American women starring at Wimbledon in recent decades have included Billie Jean King, Chris Evert, and Martina Navratilova.

Politics

From 1789 until 1917, there were no women in the U.S. Congress. In 1920, there were still none; in 1930, there were 9; in 1950, there were 10; in 1970, there were 11; in 1980, there were 17; in 1990, there were 31; in 2000, there were 65; and as of this writing, there are 73. This looks like a trend. . . .

There are also currently a record 8 women who are governors of states (in 1974, there were only 3), 17 serving as lieutenant governors; and 1,656 women are state legislators (in 1975 there were 610). A woman, Geraldine Ferraro, has run for the office of vice president, while Senator Hillary Rodham Clinton, a favorite among Democrats, appears to have her eye on the office of President. Undoubtedly, part of this incredible progress is because there are more female than male voters, and because women are more likely to turn out and vote on Election Days.

Although not an elected official, an African American woman, Dr. Condoleezza Rice, is the President's national security advisor, the highest-ranking foreign policy official after the secretary of state; in addition, three women serve in President Bush's cabinet. And Justices Ruth Bader Ginsburg and Sandra Day O'Connor have never been wallflowers about expressing their opinions while serving on the U.S. Supreme Court.

Jody Newman, of the National Women's Political Caucus, has analyzed a massive database of election records over the past 25 years. Her findings? The reason why there aren't even more women in public office isn't because women don't win elections, but because they're less likely to run in the first place.

To describe the United States as a country where gender oppression operates in the political arena is to ignore the fundamental data on women's progress.

Women's Health

*"Women are invisible in the health care system beyond
their reproductive systems. The medical model using male science,
male body, male culture, is still the norm. Women die unnecessarily
due to this male perspective."*
— Foundation for Women's Health, 1996

Are women fairly treated in the medical system of the United States? To be sure, there are problems here, as anyone who's been a patient in this country can attest to. But is it worse for women than for men, as is so often charged?

One oft-heard complaint is that women are inadequately represented in clinical trials for new medical treatments. A new drug might not work on you if you're a woman because the drug companies (a synonym for *evil* in the liberals' dictionary) never bothered to test it on women. Of course, men are physically very different from women—from Mars, as it were.

The complete lack of substantiation for this claim is fully discussed by Sally Satel, M.D., in her book, *PC, M.D.* In fact, pharmaceutical companies and government agencies such as the National Institutes of Health (NIH) routinely include women in clinical trials that test the effectiveness of medications. Even back in 1979, more than 90 percent of all NIH-funded clinical trials included women's bodies, themselves; while today, women represent more than 60 percent of all subjects in government-funded clinical trials. Where's the discrimination?

There are other sad examples of feminists trading in false health statistics. As Christina Hoff Sommers explained in *Who Stole Feminism?*, once Gloria Steinem announced that "in this country alone, 150,000 females die of anorexia each year," the figure rapidly spread through books like Naomi Wolf's *The Beauty Myth* and Myra and David Sadker's *Failing at Fairness*. It crashed into college textbooks, and Ann Landers even cited it. What's the actual figure? The Centers for Disease Control and Prevention puts the number at around 100 cases per year. One is too many, but 100 is far fewer than 150,000, and it puts a different perspective on anorexia from a public health point of view.

Another famous piece of feminist pseudoscience was the silicone-breast-implant scare; or the threat that out of a pathetic desire to self-objectify and make themselves desirable in the eyes of the oppressor, women had subjected themselves first to the surgeon's knife and then to serious health problems later on. However much the trial lawyers may have benefited, research has never shown any meaningful increased risk of autoimmune disease from breast implants. Despite the fact that this was a completely unscientific allegation against the medical community, more than $3 billion was extorted from Dow Corning in the settlement. This is a familiar tactic in the war against America: Critics generate hysteria based on false statistics and pseudoscience, and then use their claims to victimhood to exact real money based on false numbers, and this real extortion hurts real people.

Domestic Violence

Any amount of domestic violence is too much—fear and abuse have no place in the American home, period. But hysteria and false data about the subject don't help anybody. Richard Gelles, dean of the University of Pennsylvania's School of Social Work, and a longstanding researcher in the area, has compiled a list of "Understanding Domestic Violence Factoids" (http://www.mincava.umn.edu/documents/factoid/factoid.html) that are routinely recycled through the media:

- Domestic violence is the leading cause of injury to women between the ages of 15 and 44 in the United States—more than car accidents, muggings, and rapes combined *(Authors' note: this was based on a small survey from one emergency room, and the suggestion that domestic violence caused more injuries than accidents, muggings, and rapes was conjectural.)*

- The March of Dimes reports that battering during pregnancy is the leading cause of birth defects and infant mortality. *(There is no such study.)*

- Family violence has killed more women in the last five years than the total number of Americans who were killed in the Vietnam War *(55,000 were killed in Vietnam; about 1,500 women are killed by husbands and boyfriends each year).*

- Women who kill their batterers receive longer prison sentences than men who kill their partners *(average prison sentence for men who kill their wives: 17.5 years; for women who kill their husbands: 6.2 years).*

- Nationally, 50 percent of all homeless women and children are on the streets because of violence in the home. *(There is no evidence for this assertion.)*

Despite the fact that these allegations (and others like them) are either exaggerated or unsubstantiated, they have acquired a life of their own and may never die. Who can forget 1993's Super Bowl, when the public was warned of the supposed terrible 40 percent rise in domestic battery on Super Bowl Sunday, and NBC cautioned its male viewers to remain calm and in control? Eventually the *American Journalism Review* investigated the story and found that there was no data to support this claim. But it lives on in the popular imagination.

While feminists want to give America a black eye and portray the average guy as a barely repressed homicidal rapist, the reality is otherwise. When Massachusetts linked up its civil restraining order database to its criminal offender database in 1992, it found that almost 80 percent of men with restraining orders against them had prior criminal records. There's undoubtedly a small subsection of American men who are psychopathically violent and whom women would be well-advised to avoid, but even here the violence isn't gender-based: Statistics show that they're just as likely to be violent with other males.

The exaggeration of these claims is noteworthy. Somebody here certainly wants to beat up someone, but false allegations that only serve to generate fear and paranoia don't help any of us.

Opportunity, Not Oppression

To sum up, the story of American women isn't what we hear from Gloria Steinem and Andrea Dworkin in their upper-class perches, or from the Ivy League Women's Studies departments. The real story is the astounding progress of females in modern America and the happy truth that once the doors of opportunity opened, women have rushed through to success at a glorious pace in every field of endeavor. Opportunity, not oppression, is the story of women's rights in our country.

★★★ ★★★

Environmentalism

*"Needles, dead dolphins, and oil-soaked birds—are all
these signs that the shores of our familiar world are fast eroding,
that we are now standing on some new beach, facing dangers
beyond the edge of what we are capable of imagining?"*
— **Al Gore,** *Earth in the Balance,* 1992

*". . . if we don't overthrow capitalism, we don't have a
chance of saving the world ecologically. I think it is possible to
have an ecologically sound society under socialism. I don't think
it's possible under capitalism."*
— **Judi Bari,** Earth First!, 1992

*"The collective needs of non-human species must
take precedence over the needs and desires of humans."*
— **Dr. Reed F. Noss,** *The Wildlands Project,* 1992

"While the death of young men in war is unfortunate, it is no more serious than the touching of mountains and wilderness areas by humankind."
— **David Brower,** founder of Friends of the Earth; former executive director of the Sierra Club, 1993

"The forecast from Hell: Why America may see more killer tornadoes and floods, hurricanes and wildfires in the years ahead. . . . Good evening. There are new and dire predictions tonight about the future of our planet. Around the world, glaciers are in full retreat. Some, like the ancient ice cap on Mt. Kilimanjaro in Africa, could be gone in a decade or two. It's a dramatic symptom of the warming of the Earth detailed in a new thousand-page United Nations report, Climate Change 2001. It predicts the new century will bring, and I quote, 'Large-scale, and possibly irreversible, changes affecting every last person on Earth.'"
— **Dan Rather,** CBS Evening News, February 19, 2001

"United Nations studies reveal the Earth's environment is still in decline. So the leaders of every major industrial country will be in Johannesburg next week, except for George W. Bush. That makes his core constituents quite happy: representatives of the religious right, conservative activists, and big companies like ExxonMobil wrote the President this week praising him for not going to the summit. They also asked him to make sure American officials . . . keep the issue of global warming off the table. It's all part of a pattern. The Bush administration is carrying on what The Los Angeles Times this week called 'the most concerted exploitation of the public's land, air, and water since fundamental protection laws went into effect three decades ago.'"
— **Bill Moyers,** PBS's Now, August 23, 2002

"I'd say the chances are about 50-50 that humanity will be extinct or nearly extinct within 50 years. Weapons of mass destruction, disease—I mean this global warming is scaring the living daylights out of me."
— **Ted Turner,** September 27, 2003

"We have wished, we ecofreaks, for a disaster or for a social change to come and bomb us into the Stone Age, where we might live like Indians in our valley, with our localism, our appropriate technology, our gardens, our homemade religion—guilt-free at last!"
— **Stewart Brand,** *Whole Earth Catalog,* 1968

"We must make this an insecure and inhospitable place for capitalists and their projects. . . . We must reclaim the roads and plowed land, halt dam construction, tear down existing dams, free shackled rivers and return to wilderness tens of millions of acres of presently settled land."
— **Dave Foreman,** founder of Earth First!, 1992

"In ten years, all important animal life in the sea will be extinct. Large areas of coastline will have to be evacuated because of the stench of dead fish."
— **Paul Ehrlich,** Earth Day 1970

With Marxism in decline everywhere but inside the halls of academe, a pagan religion has been summoned to fill the emotional void left inside the control freak seeking a moral justification for his rage and lust for power: environmentalism. It's fascinating to note that in some ways this movement is a revival of the pre-Christian Mediterranean and Celtic mystery cults in which people worshiped the sun, the earth, trees, rivers, lakes, and rocks as gods in themselves. One need only mention the Druids of ancient England and Wales, who made human sacrifices to trees, to make the point. . . .

At its core, the environmental movement hijacks the unassailable (and one might say, obvious) belief that clean water and air are better than polluted resources, and turns it into a supermoral crusade—a grab for power by special-interest groups in the name of science and saving baby seals.

Now what could be more important than saving life on earth? What kind of savage beasts and capitalist swine would object to such a beneficent goal? Surely only subhumans of reactionary tendencies who don't deserve room on Spaceship Earth. But to see what the movement is largely—although by no means entirely—about, keep in mind one fact: Whenever people make an appeal to necessity or ethics, they're usually asking you to give them money or power or both.

The great Nordic playwright Henrik Ibsen laid out the basic environmentalist template in *An Enemy of the People* in 1882. In the play, Dr. Thomas Stockman discovers that the water in his town's celebrated mineral baths is contaminated, so he proposes closing them for two years to make the necessary repairs. The local commercial powers, threatened by the loss of revenue, stop him. By Act V, fired from his post and ostracized by the community, he determines to start a radical new school to teach young street urchins the truth about the world, vowing to "exterminate" the party leaders who have oppressed him.

This theme has been a staple of fiction ever since. Superman's father, the scientist Jor-El, discovered that Krypton was about to explode, but he was laughed at by the shortsighted, status quo-loving Kryptonian ruling council. Naturally, Jor-El was right, and he and Lara were barely able to blast their son Kal-El (as Superman was then called) off to earth in a rocket ship before the end came. *Jaws* tells the same story: The sheriff determines that there's a man-eating shark problem at Amity Island but gets over-ruled by the mayor and chamber of commerce; sure enough, pretty soon tourists are getting served up for chum.

The brilliant, morally superior person who has the key insight that corrupt businesspeople and politicians are too self-ish to admit, and who's ignored but then proven right (after it's too late), is a cliché of narrative and dramatic fiction. Of course, if Erin Brockovich is wrong, it's not much of a story—we'd want our money back after seeing a movie like that.

A Brief History of Environmentalism

It was actually a Republican, Teddy Roosevelt, who started the modern environmental movement. Roosevelt put forth a series of measures to establish the USDA Forest Service, adding 150 million acres to the country's forest reserves—including five national parks, 51 wildlife refuges, and 150 national forests. Conservatives favor conservation. Roosevelt wrote romanti-cally of "the strong attraction of the silent places, of the large tropic moons, and the splendor of the new stars; where the wan-derer sees the awful glory of sunrise and sunset in the wide waste spaces of the earth, unworn of man, and changed only by the slow change of the ages through time everlasting." And he felt such places ought to be preserved for Americans to enjoy.

The more recent "green" crusade began with several books that form a circular literature on the subject. The first of these was Rachel Carson's ominously titled 1962 bestseller, *Silent Spring,* which forecast a world where spring might arrive with no more robins left to sing, thanks to DDT and other pesticides that were working their way up the food chain. Next, Paul Ehrlich penned *The Population Bomb* in 1968, which claimed that since population grew geometrically while food supplies grew arithmetically, mass starvation was destined to kill hundreds of millions of people in the coming decade. Then *The Limits to Growth: a Report for the Club of Rome's Project on the Predicament of Mankind* by Donella Meadows appeared in 1972, alerting us that we were in imminent danger of using up all the planet's natural resources (including food) and that the only way to avert this catastrophe was for an elite group of "statesmen, policy makers, and scientists" (conveniently like the Strangelovian Club of Rome itself) to take control of the planet and restrict industrial output immediately. Hundreds of books followed in this tradition, with Al Gore's *Earth in the Balance* being one of the better-known.

As we see from the unfulfilled promises of disaster in many of the above, environmentalism has often been carried to ridiculous extremes. But environmental issues in reasonable doses are extremely sensible. No rational person can fail to be moved by the need to protect the beautiful places of the earth, as well as the resources on which life depends. Here it's worth noting that the most effective environmental crusader of the postwar period by far was Richard Nixon, who created the Environmental Protection Agency (EPA) and the Council on Environmental Quality. Nixon made environmental regulation and cleanup a federal priority on a scale undreamed of by any other President.

Perhaps because of Nixon, none of these doomsday scenarios ever happened. The predictions of disaster went down like ducks at a shooting gallery. This outcome had itself been foretold by more sensible minds. In 1980, economist Julian Simon offered Paul Ehrlich a bet. Ehrlich, like the Club of Rome, was predicting massive shortages in natural resources such as basic metals. Under the terms of the bet, Ehrlich could pick any five metals he liked, worth a total of $1,000. Ten years later, if the price of the metals had risen—that is, if the metals had become scarce—Ehrlich would win, and Simon would write him a check for the difference. If, however, the value of the metals was then less than $1,000, Ehrlich would write a check to Simon for the amount of the shortfall. Note that the bet wasn't symmetrical: Simon was virtually taking on an infinite amount of risk, as the metals could have shot up to any price, while Ehrlich's downside risk was limited to $1,000, in the extremely unlikely event the price of the metals dropped to zero. Ehrlich took the bet, choosing the vital metals copper, chrome, nickel, tin, and tungsten. Ten years later, he sent Simon a check for $576.07.

With robins in abundance, human beings well fed, and industrial materials plentiful, one might think that the environmental movement had been discredited. Far from it—instead, the books mentioned above set in motion a generation of idealists whose cause was passé before they began and who were now belatedly bent on saving us from ourselves. They created an agenda to transform the world to make it just the way they liked it, hitched to a political agenda to get us there at any cost—and with them in charge, naturally.

Let's look at some of the issues that are regularly trotted out by today's environmentalists. (The following nickel tour is suggestive but by no means exhaustive.)

Global Warming

"About 10 million residents of Bangladesh will lose their homes and means of sustenance because of the rising sea level, due to global warming, in the next few decades. Where will they go?"
— **Al Gore,** Earth in the Balance

The theory of global warming holds that, due to the emissions from our burning of fossil fuels, the amount of carbon dioxide in our atmosphere is increasing. This in turn traps more thermal radiation from the sun, heating up the planet little by little—but enough to where the polar ice caps will eventually melt, oceans will rise, and mass cataclysms will ensue. The apparent urgency of the problem was sketched in Al Gore's new foreword to his aforementioned manifesto:

> As record floods alternate with record ice-storms, as record-breaking hot months are followed by even hotter months a year later, who can afford to wait? The U.S. took the lead in convincing other nations that a voluntary international agreement to reduce carbon pollution was no longer enough—that we needed to negotiate a binding timetable to meet specific goals. When I led the U.S. delegation to the Kyoto Conference in 1997, we worked with 180 other nations to put the world on track to reduce the carbon pollution pouring into the atmosphere. The Kyoto agreement isn't the final answer to global warming, but it is the indispensable first step.

The Kyoto agreement would have required the leading industrial nations to reduce their greenhouse-gas emissions levels to below their 1990 levels by the year 2012. This reduction would have been required in spite of population changes or economic developments within the signatory countries, which included industrial countries like, say, the United States, but not, repeat *not*, the twin Asian industrial powerhouses of China and India. It would have had dire consequences for the economy of the United States, while imposing almost no limits on the worst polluters of the 21st century, such as China, India, Brazil, Thailand, and other developing nations.

Now, the third world has already given us the "brown cloud" over Asia: A two-mile-thick blanket of aerosols, soot, and ash extending from Afghanistan to over Pakistan and the Indian subcontinent, into Southeast Asia and China. This cloud cuts out sunlight and drops acid rain on the crops below and on the forests of the United States and Canada. Again, Kyoto gave these countries a pass. For this reason, many scientists questioned whether the agreement would have had any effect on global-warming rates, the treaty's *raison d'être* in the first place.

In other words, the Kyoto agreement would have been disastrous for the economy of the United States, placing it into even more of a straitjacket than it's in because of other regulations, while it would have given a blank check to the superpolluters of Asia and South America.

President Bush rightly repudiated this grossly unfair treaty in the spring of 2001; after which, Friends of the Earth blanketed the White House with 150,000 e-mails informing him that the CO_2 coming from the United States was causing climate changes around the world, leaving people to suffer from floods and hurricanes, and they warned him that future generations would never forgive this "betrayal."

At this juncture, we might well ask: What's the science behind global warming?

Taking Earth's Temperature

Although the earth is billions of years old, Galileo didn't invent his "thermoscope" until the 1590s. There weren't reliable thermometers scattered over the globe in sufficient array to give us anything like generalizable data until the latter half of the 19th century (at the earliest). Assuming that these readings are reliable, which they may or may not be, the surface of the earth is apparently warmer today than it was then. The problem becomes this: What do data points 100 years apart tell us about climate changes over the last 11,000 years, or since the end of the last ice age?

Obviously, we need to put these data in some kind of context. But to get longer-term measurements, we have to turn to ordinal-scale thermometers—tree rings, coral reefs, or ice-core samples—readings that are considerably less precise. We also have to accept that there's a large range of possible error in these rough measurement scales, as they're gathered from places widely separated in time and distance from one another. If we decide to believe this data, it tells us that the world was a warm place around the end of the first millennium, and then it cooled off considerably until 1800. Starting from what was apparently the coldest century on record, how surprising is it, then, that temperatures might be regressing upwards? Might this regression to the mean be part of how nature's thermostat operates? Even the National Academy of Sciences report on global warming in June 2001 admits that "we cannot rule out that some significant part of these changes are also a reflection of natural variability."

A third source of data—this time of high quality—comes from orbiting satellites that measure the upper atmosphere, a region that's extremely susceptible to vagaries in temperature. These have been in place since late 1978, which means that by now we have nearly a quarter century of data. Their measurements, published by Christy et al. in the 2003 *Journal of Atmospheric and Oceanic Technology,* show a warming trend of +0.06 degrees centigrade per decade over this period—vastly less than some would have guessed and well within hypotheses of natural variations.

In other words, the historical data on global warming is inchoate and incomplete.

Scientists have created computer models that attempt to simulate how the environment works. The problem is that the map is not the territory—computer models, however elaborate, are crude when it comes to simulating the almost infinitely intricate processes of nature. A computer simulation performed at

MIT by Jay Forrester was the basis for the Club of Rome report that predicted we'd run out of our most essential commodities by the 1990s. The great thing about computer models is that you can use them to prove anything you want (or, "Garbage in, garbage out," as the mantra goes).

If you're a young ecoscientist playing with a computer model, and you have 60 variables that interact to supposedly predict global warming, then you have the problem of "sensitive dependence on initial conditions," both for the values you input and the algorithms that describe how their various feedback loops interact. The assumptions you make determine your outcome. If you get a finding of no global warming, that's not very interesting. That doesn't get your name in *The New York Times,* make you a big shot to your girl- or boyfriend, or lead to new government funding or a promotion within your peer group (who are all sitting at their multifactorial computer models facing the same dilemmas—and are ready to replace your boring findings that nothing bad is happening with dramatic horror stories that get them quoted in *The New Yorker*). After all, if global warming isn't such a big deal, then *you're* really not such a big deal either. Your grants might be cancelled, and the money shuffled off to cancer research.

Since these models inevitably take a certain amount of fine-tuning (running simulations, throwing out obviously impossible outcomes, changing the equations, rerunning them, and so on), there must be a temptation, even unconsciously, to tweak the numbers ever so slightly until the ecoscientists get the finding they were looking for in the first place—the one that makes them famous, loved, rich, and important, bringing smiles to the people who pay their salaries. So we may very well ask: Are they pulling a rabbit out of a hat, or did they place the rabbit inside the hat to begin with?

Interestingly, there's no scientific uniformity of opinion that human activity increases the rate of global warming. The consensus is that greenhouse gases probably make some contribution, but the extent is unknown. In one vital way, carbon dioxide is plant food, not a pollutant. At what levels does it do more harm than good? We don't know.

What we have is a disconnect between the science, which is indeterminate and tentative, and the politics, which are zealous, uncompromising, and impose astronomical costs throughout the world, thus opening the door wide for every conceivable special-interest group. In the end, if the environmentalists have their way, the greatest burden will fall on the world's poor, as the beneficent process of globalization grinds to a halt in the face of stratospheric costs. Here we have another case where some people are using a flawed moral argument to try to take control over other people's lives.

Clearly, we need more science and less politics. The effect of the new knowledge accumulated over the last decade has been to increase our uncertainty regarding global warming, not to verify the doomsayers' catastrophic fantasies. As economist Thomas Schelling has noted, the speed at which we move toward acceptable atmospheric concentrations of greenhouse gases makes little difference as a climatic matter, but it makes a tremendous difference as an economic matter. In the meantime, Starship Earth is nothing if not resilient, and we'll be in a better position to act if we have a better understanding of the problem (if there is a problem). At that point, the special-interest politics inherent to emissions controls will have to bow to the greater glory of science.

For the present, there's no reason to assume other than that the planet will continue to warm another degree or two over the coming century, and the oceans will rise by six to ten inches—all business as usual for a planet whose background climate is constantly changing anyway. One is tempted to speculate that the environmentalists have projected their inner sense of guilt on to the world at large, and are seeking their personal redemption by redeeming the planet instead of themselves. Or that this is just another effort for people of no special significance—which is all of us—to create a world historical model that makes them important. But what we have after all our hypothesizing is done is often a leftist/environmentalist power grab, or an attempt to impose strict regulations on human freedom at titanic costs to prevent a catastrophe that's very likely not happening in the first place.

Oh, by the way, remember those terrifying stories in *The New York Times* about Antarctica melting? Guess what—it's not. The temperature of the continent has been declining over the past 25 years, and the extent of ice there is increasing (Doran et al., *Nature*, January 2002).

Ehrlich's Population Bomb

> *"[T]he battle to feed humanity is over. In the 1970s the world population will undergo famines—hundreds of millions of people are going to starve to death in spite of any crash programs embarked upon now."*
> — **Paul Ehrlich,** The Population Bomb

Is the world's population growing so fast that we're heading for disaster? This argument has been made since Thomas Malthus's "An Essay on the Principle of Population" in 1798. Malthus saw that plants and animals produce far more offspring than actually survive, and he connected the dots to see that human beings did this as well. He claimed that unless family size was regulated, we'd reach a point where the human race would run out of food, leading to famine on a global scale. This, again, came from the premise that population grows geometrically, or exponentially, while food production grows arithmetically.

In *The Population Bomb,* Paul Ehrlich pushed this premise to hysterical hyperbole. Here's the money quote: "Just remember that, at the current growth rate, in a few thousand years everything in the visible universe would be converted into people, and the ball of people would be expanding at the speed of light." This is truly a preposterous utterance for a Stanford University professor (or maybe that's how people get to be professors in today's world). In fact, today the world faces the opposite scenario: population shrinkage.

According to the United Nations 2002 report of *World Population Prospects,* the average birthrate in this century now looks like it's heading toward 1.85 per woman; in 1950, it was 5 births per woman. (To just sustain population levels, a birthrate of 2.1 per woman is required.) In less-developed countries, it's fallen from a mean of nearly 7 children per woman in 1950 to 3 today; more developed countries, like Europe and Japan, will see their rate plummet to 1.3 births per woman, leading to incredible shrinking populations and a huge burden of older people without an adequate native workforce to pay for them.

The United States will continue to grow, with a birthrate at population-sustaining levels; longer-lived senior citizens; and a tremendous influx of immigrants, many of whom incomprehensibly risk life and limb to come to this fascistic anti-human Bush/Cheney dictatorship. According to the *International Migration Report* of the United Nations, the U.S. already takes in more immigrants than the rest of the world combined, in spite of the truth that's well known in university coffeehouses and at *The Nation*—that this country is in reality a hell of reactionary, monopolizing, capitalist exploitation.

The world population now looks like it will top out at around 8 billion people by midcentury, instead of the 10 or 11 billion foreseen earlier. This figure portends growing affluence, as breadwinners are able to provide more education for each child. People can now raise fewer, better-quality children; that is, no longer do we need large families to work the farm, nor do we need to deal with the contingency of several children dying due to smallpox, cholera, typhoid, and typhus. Another benefit: When people have fewer children, they're less likely to march them off to war. All in all, this is a far less dire future than the population explosionists were predicting.

To put these numbers in context, recall that the population of the planet grew from 1.6 billion in 1900 to more than 6 billion today. This growth spurt occurred because of advances in medicine that have wiped out many of the infectious diseases that were the leading cause of early death—not because people started having more babies. As Nicholas Eberstadt of the Harvard Center for Population and Developmental Studies notes, the 20th century witnessed not only a population explosion, but also a health explosion and a prosperity explosion.

According to economic historian Angus Maddison, while the world's population increased fourfold, its real per capita gross domestic product (GDP) rose even more. World economic output at the end of the 20th century was roughly 18 times what it was at the beginning, and the prices of most basic commodities fell significantly. Yet *The Limits to Growth* prophesied that the world would run out of gold in 1981, silver and mercury in 1985, and zinc in 1990.

★ ★ ★

The world's population will continue to increase through the first half of the 21st century; yet, thanks to advances in agricultural biotechnology, it will be possible to feed everyone using existing farmland at lower prices. While earth-aware shoppers at the Santa Monica, California, farmers' market may prefer organic baby peas and carrots, the truth is that organic methods are a luxury for the rich and would produce mass starvation if employed for all. Mass agribusiness farming is far more earth friendly in reality, as it makes the most efficient use of resources such as fertilizer, water, and land.

Of course, environmental extremists are opposed. They even want to keep scientifically engineered seeds, fertilizers, and pesticides out of the hands of farmers in sub-Saharan Africa, where the likely alternative is starvation. Why? No one knows. (Our guess is infantile obstructionism, the exact same phenomenon as when a small child refuses to do what his parents want, just to show who's boss, but we emphasize this is a guess.) There's no proven harm from these genetically engineered products, balanced against enormous proven benefits. This is worth pausing to consider. Purely on the basis of superstition or some infantile wish to call attention to their own moral "superiority," environmentalists would doom millions to hunger, while the big drug and chemical companies—completely maligned in the press—are responsible for keeping hundreds of millions of people alive and well fed.

For example, as Michael Fumento notes in *Bioevolution,* one-third of the world's population is estimated to be anemic (especially women), and one-fifth of all starvation deaths are caused by a lack of iron, largely because rice-based diets are iron deficient. Rice is actually loaded with iron, but a molecule called phytate prevents it from being absorbed. Bioengineers have found a gene that breaks down the phytate and allows the iron to be assimilated—the result will be improved nutrition for billions of people.

We've entered looking-glass land here. Mass starvation is essentially a political, not an agricultural, phenomenon. It's either deliberate (as with Stalin in Ukraine and Pol Pot in Cambodia), or an artifact of a central planned economy whose rulers claim to know best and never do. Major famines are unknown in modern democracies in the 20th and 21st centuries.

Pollution

> *"Almost half of all American rivers, lakes, and creeks are damaged or threatened by water pollution."*
> — **Al Gore,** *Earth in the Balance*

London had serious air-pollution problems dating back to the 13th century due to the black soot and smoke from burning coal. Consequently, King Edward I established the world's first air-pollution commission in 1272. Environmental activist Robert F. Kennedy, Jr., writes with relish in *Rolling Stone* (12/11/2003) how the king "made it a capital offense to burn coal in London, and violators were executed for the crime." Oh, for the good old days! Predictably, the edict was completely ignored, since there was no affordable alternative to provide heat.

Nixon's EPA, however much inclined to overreach, at least has had better results where air and water are concerned. Air pollution has declined 25 percent over the past 30 years, doing so even while we experienced large increases in the population, GDP, and vehicle miles traveled (see Figure 5.1 on next page).

949457

Figure 5.1: Percentage of Change in Motor Vehicle Emissions Related to Demographics and Transportation 1970–1999

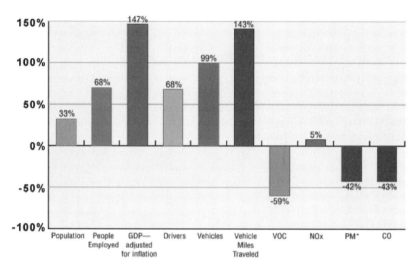

Note: *VOC = Volatile Organic Compounds, NOx = Nitrogen Oxides, PM = Particulate Matter, CO = Carbon Monoxides.* **Source:** *Federal Highway Commission*

Air quality will automatically get progressively better in the years ahead, as aging vehicles are replaced with newer, more fuel-efficient, and less polluting models.

The water we drink today is vastly cleaner than what people consumed 100 years ago, when contaminants in drinking water were a common cause of death. The Cuyahoga River, which flows through the downtown of Dennis Kucinich's Cleveland, was so polluted in 1969 that it caught fire—today, it's been cleaned up, and even the fish have returned. A glass of water from the Potomac River used to be a meal in itself, but no longer. As American Enterprise Institute President Christopher DeMuth (and brother of one of your authors) has pointed out, as far as man-made pollution goes, we have it within our technological power to attain any degree of air and water purity we wish. The only questions are political and economic: How much of society's resources do we want to expend in this direction, versus other goals we might to pursue (like driving automobiles or heating our homes)?

There is a serious problem with pollution in today's world; however, as we previously noted, it's not coming from the United States. America has some of the strictest environmental regulations and most up-to-date anti-pollution technology there is. The offenders today are third-world countries, where rapid industrial development is unaccompanied by environmental regulation. If the environmentalists want to do some good, they should demonstrate in New Delhi, Brasilia, and especially Beijing, where they should wear Kevlar vests just to be safe.

*** *

To give credit where it's due, Adolf Hitler deserves the prize for being the strictest eco-aware ruler of the 20th century. Hitler's concern for purity extended far beyond the Aryan race: He was an organic vegetarian and a rabid anti-smoker, and his love for the Fatherland led him to incorporate earlier German critiques of deforestation, consumerism, urban sprawl, Christianity, and capitalism into Nazism. It's no accident that *Triumph of the Will* and *The Olympiad,* two fine documentaries by another great environmentalist, Leni Riefenstahl (a genuine guru to many in the environmental movement despite her slavish devotion to Hitler; she was recently applauded at the Academy Awards), show vigorous, naked young men getting healthy exercise in the open air as a backdrop. The Führer was also obsessed with protecting the forests, rivers, and mountains of *Das Reich* against Jewish industrial pollution. Environmentalism doesn't always go hand in hand with good mental health or desirable social policy, although we hasten to add that it sometimes does.

Sustainable Development

> *"A continuously expanding global economy is slowly*
> *destroying its host—the Earth's ecosystem."*
> **— Worldwatch Institute,** 1998

Apparently, in modern America, Democrats are the only ones who want sustainable development. Since no one with children would ever wish future generations to do without the advantages we take for granted today, what's the point of this qualifier? Well, what *sustainable* really means (surprise, surprise) is "controlled by the state." That way, commissars can slow it down or stop it before it gets out of control and harms the environment. Government oversight, as always, will ensure that no one gets hurt.

In this view, property rights, once thought essential to economic growth (John Adams considered them to be as sacred as the laws of God), must take a backseat to government agencies that can seize your property and tell you what to do with it if, for example, some endangered species shows up. Formerly, nature embraced a Darwinian struggle, where species came and went according to their fitness, but now environmentalists want to stop the clock and give all living species an affirmative-action ticket to immortality. Presently there are 1,263 endangered species, with thousands more on the wait list. For a species, this is like getting into Harvard.

While we all want to save those cuddly creatures with big brown eyes, we may be less concerned about stinging and biting insects. We may want to save the ones that cost other people money while feeling less compassion toward the ones that cost *us* money. For example, when eight endangered flies were found on land proposed for a new hospital in San Bernardino County, the Fish and Wildlife Service forced the hospital to move construction 350 feet and set aside two acres of dune land for the flies—they ended up spending enough money to treat 23,644 outpatients to save them (*The Wall Street Journal*, 2/11/1997). Unfortunately, these kinds of examples can be multiplied, as environmentalism and the protection of species don't come free.

If the government decides that progress must stop because some resource might be becoming scarce, the question arises as to how they know what needs to be protected and how much protection it needs. Traditionally, this function is supplied by the price system in an open market. Due to supply and demand, when supplies are low, this is reflected in an increased price, which lowers demand until a new equilibrium is reached. Under Communism, the theory was that the state's elite corps of central planners could do a better job of allocating resources than the open market could; and as everyone knows, this proved a disaster. Now, using the smoke screen of environmentalism, the state (and the people who will be white knights in the struggle for Mother Earth, thus elevating themselves above waiting tables at an eco-friendly café) wants another chance.

Artificial Chemicals and Bioengineering

We've always had difficulty with people who say that they're against chemicals, insofar as the list of material things that aren't made out of them is extremely short. Evidently, there's something about "man-made" chemicals that bears the imprint of original sin: The strings, quarks, atoms, and molecules that make them up are somehow different from all the others that came out of the big bang. We're just not sure how.

Rachel Carson's *Silent Spring* was the first to sound the alarm, predicting a cancer plague that would sweep the land. This hasn't happened; in fact, the rise in the prevalence of cancer is really an artifact of the tremendous strides made in eliminating other causes of death. In 1900, when the average life expectancy was 48 years, most people didn't live long enough to die of cancer or heart disease, which are often diseases of old age.

Carson was especially riled up about the pesticide DDT, which environmentalists have now been successful in getting banned throughout the world, to the great relief of mosquitoes everywhere. DDT is history—long live the mosquito! In some parts of the world, malaria rates have skyrocketed, and the net effect of the ban has been decidedly negative. As Dr. Michael Crichton informed the Commonwealth Club in 2003:

> DDT is not a carcinogen, did not cause birds to die, and should never have been banned. I can tell you that the people who banned it knew that it wasn't carcinogenic and banned it anyway. I can tell you that the DDT ban has caused the deaths of tens of millions of poor people, mostly children, whose deaths are directly attributable to a callous, technologically advanced Western society that promoted the new cause of environmentalism by pushing a fantasy about a pesticide, and thus irrevocably harmed the third world. Banning DDT is one of the most disgraceful episodes in the 20th-century history of America.

Today, greens are trying to ban the pesticide paraquat (which some of our pot-smoking friends might recall), which currently protects 40 percent of the world's food supply. One can only imagine with severe dread the consequences to poor people everywhere if this campaign is successful.

According to Dennis Avery of the Hudson Institute's Center for Global Food Issues, if we were to eliminate bioengineered crops, fertilizers, herbicides, and pesticides, the world would have to appropriate an amount of land equal to the size of North America for farming in order to feed just its current population. To put the comparative magnitude of risks from bioengineered food versus other risks in perspective, Nobelist James Watson, codiscoverer of the structure of DNA, once remarked to one of your authors, "I'd rather drink a glass of recombinant DNA than let a stray dog lick my hand."

Nature has its own pollutants and poisons that are the equal of anything we can make. Mankind didn't invent the bubonic plague or smallpox. The fact that something is man-made doesn't make it bad, despite the money and power to be had by saying so. By the same token, the fact that something is natural—like a cancer cell—doesn't necessarily make it good.

Fossil Fuels

Are we running out of fossil fuels, as widely predicted in the 1970s? A look at the historical record is enlightening, as David Deming notes in his 2003 report to the National Center for Policy Analysis:

- In 1855, four years before the first oil well was drilled in the United States, an advertisement for "Kier's Rock Oil" advised consumers to "hurry, before this wonderful product is depleted from Nature's laboratory."

- In 1874, the state geologist of Pennsylvania, the nation's leading oil-producing state, estimated that there was only enough oil left in the U.S. to keep kerosene lamps burning for four years.

- In 1918, a writer in the *Oil Trade Journal* noted that in the 25 years he'd been following the oil business, he'd witnessed repeated instances of people saying that the world's supply of commercial crude oil would be exhausted within a few years.

- In May of 1920, the U.S. Geological Survey announced that the world's total endowment of oil amounted to 60 billion barrels.

According to the U.S. Department of Energy, the world still has more than a trillion barrels of oil reserves and more than five quadrillion cubic feet of natural gas, with more reserves being discovered all the time. Despite the pronouncement in *The Limits to Growth* that the world would run out of oil by 1992, we're happy to report that there's still gasoline available at the pump (at least as of this writing). This has become such a non-issue that even environmentalists have been forced to drop the scarcity argument. Now they admit that maybe we're not running out of fossil fuels—but they say we shouldn't burn them anyway, because of global warming (see above).

What about glorious, nonpolluting, infinitely renewable "alternative energy sources"? Sadly, solar power and windmills aren't quite ready for prime time. Writing in *Foreign Affairs,* Richard Rhodes and Denis Beller calculate that to use solar power for the entire planet with today's technology would require 20 percent of the world's iron reserves and cover 500,000 square miles of land. A single fuel-efficient, natural-gas, 550-megawatt power plant produces more electricity than 13,000 windmills spread over thousands of acres and provides that power at a fraction of the cost. Despite billions of tax dollars and credits lavished on research and development for renewable energy, 0.1 percent of our power comes from the sun and wind

today—a figure expected to rise to 0.25 percent by the year 2020. Alternative energy technologies are so cost ineffective that they'd disappear overnight without substantial ongoing "feel-good" subsidies.

Garbage and Recycling

"The waste crisis is integrally related to the crisis of industrial civilization as a whole. Just as our internal combustion engines have automated the process by which our lungs transform oxygen into carbon dioxide, our industrial apparatus has vastly magnified the process by which our digestive system transforms raw material into human energy and growth—and waste."
— **Al Gore,** *Earth in the Balance*

There are undoubtedly many things to worry about in life, but where to put the garbage isn't one of them. As Daniel Benjamin of the Property and Environment Research Center has calculated, if we permitted our rubbish to grow to the height of New York City's famous Fresh Kills Landfill (225 feet), a site only about ten miles on a side could hold all of America's garbage for the next century.

All that packaging we use to wrap our products? It's a good thing: It reduces spoilage and breakage, and lets us transport goods to market cheaply, using less fuel. And all that curbside recycling? Apart from making us feel virtuous (although that itself is possibly of some value), it's considered a joke even by environmentalists. According to the Congressional Office of Technology Assessment, it's "not clear whether secondary manufacturing [i.e., recycling] produces less pollution per ton of material processed than primary manufacturing" does in the first place.

Meanwhile, curbside recycling requires that more trucks be used to collect the same amount of waste materials. In your authors' beloved city of Los Angeles, the city estimates that due to curbside recycling, its fleet of trucks is twice as large as it otherwise would be (800 vs. 400 trucks). Needless to say, this is just what we need in L.A.: a lot more trucks on the street. The Property and Environmental Research Center concludes that curbside recycling is so expensive that it costs between 35 and 55 percent more than simply throwing something away.

Paradoxical Effects

The environmentalists' agenda has reached a point not only of diminishing returns, but of paradoxical effects. Efforts to align themselves with governments to bring redemption to their world are unpromising. A clean environment is a good thing with a high social priority, but it must be weighed against competing goods, such as jobs, personal freedoms, the elimination of poverty, and the right to private property.

Let's close with a final example, brought to our attention by Sean Paige, an adjunct fellow at the Competitive Enterprise Institute. As regular viewers of the Discovery Channel know, sharks have acquired a bad reputation through no real fault of their own. They're really our friends. So, in 1992, under pressure from endangered species and wildlife advocacy activists, Florida banned commercial shark fishing in state waters. Following suit, in 1994 the federal government began a "shark stock rebuilding program" in the Atlantic and Gulf of Mexico (your tax dollars at work). At last, we put an end to our senseless cruelty to these benevolent creatures of the sea. And how did they respond to our kindness? Why, by turning around and biting the hand that feeds them. Florida averaged ten shark attacks per

year in the early 1990s; then the figure doubled; and for the last two years, it nearly quadrupled, with a total of 37 attacks in 2002. For events supposedly as random as shark attacks, this is developing into something that looks remarkably like a trend. Meanwhile, the same shark apologists assure us that the water's fine, there's nothing to be concerned about here. True enough—if you have three rows of razor-sharp, three-inch-long serrated teeth.

The first wave of environmentalists (primarily Republicans) picked all the low-hanging fruit; having rapidly reached the point of diminishing returns, the current bunch has now arrived at the point where their meddlesome efforts generally do more harm than good. Rigid and unreasoning environmentalism is an ideological successor to Communism in its willingness to abandon property rights and stop globalization in its tracks—one thing that seems to be doing people some good right now—in the name of achieving a higher planetary consciousness. All this merely serves to make environmentalists feel holier-than-thou while conveniently allowing them to control our lives and pocketbooks even more than they already do.

★★★ ★★★

Chapter

Conservatives

"If, as John Stuart Mill said, stupid people are generally conserva-
tive, then there are lots of conservatives we will never hire. . . .
Members of academia tend to be a bit smarter than average."
— **Robert Brandon,** Duke University biology and philosophy
professor, wildly misusing J. S. Mill to defend Duke's surveyed 148 to
8 Democratic-to-Republican faculty bias, February 10, 2004

"What you have now is people that are closet racists, misogynists,
homophobes, and people who love tilted playing fields and the
politics of exclusion identifying as conservative."
— **Janeane Garofalo,** August 18, 2003

"In South Africa, we'd call it apartheid. In Nazi Germany,
we'd call it fascism. Here we call it conservatism."
— **Jesse Jackson,** January 29, 1995

The depth of some liberals' rage and hatred toward conservatives is distressing, to say the least. This has probably always been true, and was even truer in the polarized anti-Communist days of the 1950s.

What's new, however, is an alarming trend. This trend smacks of the Stalin and Brezhnev eras' endeavor to medicalize anti-Communist thought: the effort to portray anyone who isn't a card-carrying liberal as not only corrupt, but also mentally unsound. You may think that this effort is fanciful, but we assure you that it's real.

In 2003, four university professors published an article in *Psychological Bulletin* bearing the innocuous title of "Political Conservatism as Motivated Social Cognition." Their effort was nothing less than to sum up everything psychologists have written in the last 50 years about the psychology of conservatives—a favorite topic, by the way, of left-wing psychologists. They concluded that conservatives are something fairly close to insane (*Webster's:* "mentally disordered").

Before we delve into their argument, a question springs to mind: Who paid for this research? Hiring four university professors to analyze 88 books and articles and write a 37-page treatise with hundreds of references doesn't come cheap. That amounts to thousands of pages of obscure technical reading for all four authors, plus the time to weigh and consider each of these studies, formulate their reactions, come to a consensus with colleagues across the country, and write up and edit their findings in a way that satisfied each of them in addition to the journal editors and reviewers.

Per academic custom, the authors list their sponsors on the first page, and these include the National Institute of Mental Health and the National Science Foundation. In other words, we, the taxpayers, seemingly paid for this study. According to the House Republican Study Committee, these grants to the writers added up to at least $1.2 million (and possibly more) devoted to research stigmatizing conservatives as not quite right in the head.

Curiously, when we contacted the National Institute of Mental Health and the National Science Foundation, they adamantly denied funding the study at all. We were told that they seek to do only good things with public money, like cure disease—and conservatism isn't (yet) one of the diseases on their radar. So evidently, no one paid for this study, yet 1.2 million taxpayer dollars later, there it is, an immaculate conception.

Conservatism—a Medical Condition?

According to these men of science, where does political conservatism come from? The basic desire for freedom from tyranny and oppression? A belief in free markets and limited government? No. Unlike liberals, conservatives don't see the world clearly. They view life in a fun-house mirror that distorts all of their perceptions and leads to their misbegotten political philosophy, with all of its hurtful consequences. We discover that, according to these psychologists:

- Conservatives have a morbid fear of death, so, in an attempt to manage their terror, they tend to turn to authoritarian religion. The scientists quote John Lennon and the Plastic Ono Band to the effect that "God is a concept by which we measure our pain." *(We're not kidding—this is really what their study says.)*

- Conservatives are highly dogmatic, needing a closed-end belief system to ward off anxiety.

113

*(Yes, the researchers actually say this about conserva-
tives, not socialists.)*

- Conservatives are not open to new experiences. They only want to experience the world in the safe, pre-dictable ways that they've already done in the past.

- Conservatives are intolerant of ambiguity. A fear of complexity leads them to make snap decisions, which they never question later. *(When one of your authors pointed out to the lead scientist behind this study that no one could be less "tolerant of ambiguity" than a leftist university teacher, he was informed that to even make this observation showed a lack of tolerance of ambiguity!)*

- Conservatives have a high need for order, structure, and closure.

- Conservatives have "low integrative complexity," which means that they think in simplistic, clichéd terms. Rigid, dichotomous, black-and-white think-ing is the rule. Sophisticated thinkers, they are not. See Spot run. Go, Spot, go.

- Conservatives are easily threatened and are fearful of loss; thus, they enshrine the status quo. They fear negative results from proposed social changes, instead of getting excited by the possibility of posi-tive new and exciting outcomes. This negative atti-tude makes them easily manipulated by fearmon-gering politicians. *(We're not making this up. Again, they said this about conservatives, not liberals.)*

If this weren't reason enough to make the reader of the study write a check to the Democratic National Committee or **www.moveon.org**, there's even some evidence that conservatives suffer from that psychological bubonic plague of modern life: low self-esteem. The scientists note that such a condition has been associated (by other "scientists") with racism and the tendency to marginalize out-groups. Presumably, Lenin, Mao, Stalin, Pol Pot, and other left-wingers who simply mass-murdered out-groups had high self-esteem. . . .

But on the plus side, conservatives are inclined to be neat and tidy. (Obviously, the researchers never met the authors of this book.)

If you're a conservative and fail to recognize yourself in this picture, it could be that you're too cognitively challenged or defensive to see the nose on your face. Maybe you just can't handle the truth. You see, these doctors of the soul have diagnosed conservatism as a condition motivated by a primitive need to manage fear. Conservatism isn't a political choice, like homosexuality, but is instead a kind of neurotic defense mechanism. At least we can take some solace in the authors' reassurance that conservatism isn't in itself a mental illness requiring immediate treatment. (Still, we might want to stick a psychiatrist's card up on the refrigerator with a magnet, just to be safe.)

The Diagnostic and Statistical Manual of Medical Disorders, Fourth Edition (DSM-IV) of the American Psychiatric Association—the book that psychiatrists and psychologists use to diagnose mental illness—is already a political hot potato. For example, "homosexuality" was classified as a sexual deviation in earlier editions of this manual, but in 1973, psychiatrists voted to remove it. The key word in that sentence is *vote,* an interesting method for identifying and diagnosing medical diseases. To this day, conceits such as "post-traumatic stress disorder" and "attention deficit disorder" are listed in the manual of mental disorders, as well as the catchall "adjustment reaction with mixed emotional features," which can basically refer to anything. The scientists who wrote this study have supplied ample ammunition here to include a "conservative cognitive disorder" as a diagnosable DSM-V condition, if the political winds were right (or, should we say, left).

In 1964, some 1,189 American psychiatrists reported in *Fact* magazine that Barry Goldwater wasn't psychologically fit to be President of the United States. One would have hoped that mental-health professionals had learned something from their Soviet counterparts about the wisdom of putting psychiatry at the service of politics. (*Psychiatric Terror*, by Sidney Bloch and Peter Reddaway, provides a chilling account of the use of psychiatric "hospitals" for political dissidents under Brezhnev. In earlier times, no such medical pretense was necessary: Lenin and Stalin simply shot their enemies without bothering to call them insane first.) Even now, psychiatric hospitals in China house political prisoners diagnosed with "political monomania," which is treated with electroshock therapy.

This new research on conservatives is perfect for all those who want to medicalize political beliefs such as homophobia, xenophobia, racism, and sexism. This way, the solution isn't repression, reeducation, or indoctrination; instead, it's "sensitivity training"—at least for the mild cases, for now. Liberals have always been quick to call conservatives stupid, but for leftist American psychologists to use their professional journals to "psychopathologize" conservatism (or, as we see it, something very close—but then you know how confused we are) is unfortunate in the extreme.

We don't question the researchers' intelligence, integrity, or desire to do good, but their conclusions sadly illustrate the Left's tendency to find anyone who disagrees with them to be not merely ignorant and evil, but mentally disturbed as well. There's no clear limit to this except a one-party state in which anyone not in the liberal group is considered unwell and therefore not worthy of attention. That way lies an end to freedom.

This Is Conservatism?

The paper we've been discussing runs further aground on its definition of conservatism. These scientists identify the core features of conservatism as being a *resistance to change* coupled with a *tolerance of inequality* (or, consistent with conservatives' supposedly irascible natures, perhaps that should be rephrased as an *intolerance for equality*). This makes the paper a circular Möbius strip: If this is your definition of conservatives, then how else could the paper have turned out except to discover that conservatives have these characteristics? John Ray, one of the few conservative psychologists in the profession, suggests that the scientists would have been better advised to actually talk to a conservative at the outset. Had they done so, they might have learned that conservatives are neither opposed to change nor in favor of it; rather, they're opposed to liberal change and are in favor of conservative change. The reputation conservatives have for resisting change comes from their historical record of fighting the incursions of tyrannical governments intent on appropriating the rights and liberties of individuals.

As to conservatives' other defining characteristic, their "condoning inequality in some form," there's no politician who doesn't do this in some form. Conservatives, for example, favor equality of opportunity, while liberals supposedly favor equality of outcome, which necessarily involves inequality in the treatment of persons with different levels of talent and industry.

(Whether liberals really want equality of outcome is unlikely—what they might actually want is equality of outcome with them in control.) To choose equality of outcome is to deny equality of opportunity.

Beyond this, the scientists don't appear to us to have closely read the studies they were supposed to be summarizing, although we might be mistaken. Professor James Lindgren of Northwestern University has examined all the primary research in this article, and believes that the authors have neither adequately sampled the data that exists (for instance, only two of conservative psychologist John Ray's hundreds of papers on the subject are mentioned), nor properly understood the data in front of them.

One study, for example, by Pamela Conover and Stanley Feldman, is supposed to show how conservatives hate change. But Conover and Feldman's data shows precisely the opposite: Conservatives favor changes like a flat tax, people getting ahead on their own initiative as opposed to having the government guarantee employment, people paying for medical services themselves versus having the government provide them, and so on.

Strangely, the scientists classify Stalin, Hitler, Khrushchev, Castro, Mussolini, Reagan, and Limbaugh as conservatives—supposedly because they all hated change and wanted to return to a Neverland in the past. To equate the great force for freedom in our time—Reagan—with the likes of Stalin and Hitler gives away the essentially propagandistic agenda of this enterprise. Of course, Stalin, Khrushchev, Castro, and Mussolini were all Communists, and Hitler was a socialist, all of which are at the opposite end of the political spectrum from conservatives. The scientists determine that Reagan's chief accomplishment was to "roll back both the New Deal era and the 1960s," which, as far as we've been able to determine, Reagan did not do—yet no mention is made of the small matter of his large role in winning the Cold War and setting the stage for massive liberalization in Eastern Europe, which he most assuredly did do.

✳ ✳ ✳

Are conservatives really authority-worshiping goose-steppers ready to lead America into a Fourth Reich? The scientists' most beloved measure of "authoritarianism" is the something called the Right-Wing Authoritarian Scale, and yet, as John Ray points out, high scores on this scale in the general population don't correlate with membership in any political party. Leftists are just as likely to get a high authoritarian score as rightists are.

In support of their thesis that right-wingers are nascent authoritarians, the scientists cite a number of studies that purport to show how, during crises, people turn to authoritarian religions in preference to nonauthoritarian ones. Yet a closer examination of the data by Lindgren shows that the congregations of the scientists' "authoritarian" churches were actually more liberal than those of the "nonauthoritarian churches" at the time (such as the Episcopal Church, which was then known as "the Republican party at prayer").

Speaking of blind obedience to authority, who are more likely to say that people should follow the law without exception—liberals or conservatives? According to the General Social Survey (the single most comprehensive survey that exists in America, after the U.S. Census), the highest score belongs to moderates (46 percent). While conservatives (45 percent) do score higher than liberals (33 percent), the groups that score highest of all are Asian Americans (71 percent), followed by African Americans (56 percent), both consistent liberal Democratic voting blocs. Mindless obedience to authority would hardly seem to be defining characteristic of conservatives.

Even the scientists' peripheral findings about conservatives are questionable:

- While the researchers assume that conservatives are a superstitious lot, the Gallup Poll shows that liberals are much more inclined to believe in ESP, haunted houses, reincarnation, ghosts, and astrology than conservatives. Presumably, conservatives' rejection of activities like consulting a fortune-teller is what constitutes being "closed to new experiences."

- The scientists devote a section of their paper to discussing conservatives' "Pessimism, Disgust, and Contempt," completely ignoring the fact that in the 2000 General Social Survey, extreme conservatives were a "very happy" 49 percent to extreme liberals' 30 percent. The latest Gallup Poll shows that 62 percent of Republicans report being very happy, while only 50 percent of Democrats do.

- Another section of the paper concludes that conservatives are plagued by "Fear, Anger, and Aggression," but the General Social Survey in 1996 revealed that, by a staggering margin, conservatives were much less likely to report being angry at someone every day during the past week than were extreme liberals (7 percent to 24 percent). They were also less likely to report being fearful during the past week (33 percent to 56 percent).

- While the scientists want to portray conservatives as having "low integrative complexity" (hint: this is a psychologist's way of calling someone stupid), conservative Republicans score the highest on years of education, highest degree attained, and vocabulary and analogies tests (the latter being an especially good measure of abstract integrative ability). Some famous conservatives, including William F. Buckley, Jr., George F. Will, and William Safire, have even been known to use words instead of picking up a rock to throw at their opponents.

In sum, conservatives aren't authoritarians; they're good and bad, weak and strong, and smart and stupid, just like everyone else. Attempting to define conservatism as a cognitive disorder by whatever contrivance they can is a symptom of the anger some in the Left feel against conservatives—who are the dominant political group in America—and, by extension, at America itself. This is the mark of frighteningly intolerant men and women, not of a free society, and it sets a dangerous precedent. If this attitude were somehow extended into the realm of action (such as making "conservative cognitive disorder" a mental disease under HillaryCare), there would be a sudden and sickening end to our free society.

★★★ ★★★

A Brief Digression on Republicans

"'Republican' comes in the dictionary just after 'reptile' and just above 'repugnant.'"
— **Julia Roberts,** well-known political lexicographer, September 14, 2000

"For years, the insidious and blatantly racist strategy of the Republican party has been to pit the middle classes against the lower classes, while sucking money from both groups up the economic pyramid to the smiling faces at the top."
— **Bob Herbert,** *The New York Times*, September 22, 1995

"The Republicans are the real threat. They are the real threat to our women, they are the real threat to our children, they are the real threat to the clean water, the clean air, the rich landscape in America. They are the real threat to fairness, to equality, to an enlightened Supreme Court."
— **Mario Cuomo,** August 27, 1992

*"When I listen to the Republicans in Congress on foreign policy,
there's such an 'I'm stupid and proud of it' attitude."*
— *New York Times* columnist **Thomas L. Friedman**
on *Face the Nation*, March 14, 1999

*"The new Republican majority in Congress took a big step today
on its legislative agenda to demolish or damage government-aid
programs, many of them designed to help children and the poor."*
— **Dan Rather,** *CBS Evening News*, March 16, 1995

*"The Republicans are going to be the Party That Canceled the
Clean Air Act and Took Hot Lunches from Children, the Orphan-
age Party of Large White Men Who Feel Uneasy Around Gals."*
— **Garrison Keillor,** *Time*, March 13, 1995

I n this chapter, we'd like to examine a few of the more common charges concerning Republicans, including some made
against our President.

Is the GOP Really the Party of the Rich?

If the more than 50 million Republicans who voted for
Bush in 2000 were all billionaires, our country must be far
richer than anyone knows. In fact, an awful lot of ordinary
people are voting Republican these days and always have. If
Republicans really are the rich capitalist exploiting class, then
they've done an amazing job of duping the general public into
believing otherwise. According to the Republican National
Committee, between January 2001 and September 2003, among
the 1,000,305 first-time contributors to the Republican party, the
average contribution was $29.80. The Center for Responsive

Politics reveals that during the last election cycle, two-thirds of the donations under $200 went to Republicans. By sector, Republicans drew support from across the breadth of the economy: retirees, health-care workers, insurance brokers, energy and other utility workers, bankers, manufacturers, distributors, and contractors. Evidently, the Mr. Burnses (Homer Simpson's boss on *The Simpsons*) of this world are too greedy or shortsighted to back their puppet candidates with their wallets—only 7 percent of donations over $1,000,000 went to Republicans in 2000.

The remaining 93 percent of $1,000,000-plus donations during the last presidential election went to Democrats . . . a curious set of financiers for a party that represents the little guy. In 2002, nine out of the ten largest contributions from individuals went to the Democratic party (ten out of ten if you disqualify the one donor who hedged his bets by giving to both parties). Expand this list to the 100 largest individual contributions, and you find that 79 percent of the money went to Democrats, while 21 percent went to Republicans.

Looking at the base of Democratic financial support, we don't find it spread evenly across the floor of the United States. Instead, it narrowly rises from three special-interest groups: the entertainment industry (angry Howard Dean was the darling of 90210), trial lawyers (ka-ching!), and trade unions. And while you might think that the unions represent all the working men and women in our country, this would be an error. According to the Bureau of Labor Statistics, union members constituted less than 13 percent of all wage and salaried workers in the United States in 2002, and less than 10 percent in the private sector. Union members are most heavily concentrated in one segment: the government.

Since our friend Ann Coulter demolished the myth that Republicans are tools of a "religious right" in her book *Slander*, we'll simply update her findings to note that in the 2002 election cycle, there wasn't a single religious group donating to either party among the top 100 donors. Since 1990, a total of $3,591,748 has been donated by clergy and religious groups, and this pile was split 54 percent Republican and 45 percent Democratic—a remarkably small sum, and rather evenly divided, with which to dominate the national agenda.

Meanwhile, Christians at the polls prove to be intractable: In 2000, Protestants went for Bush (55 percent) over Gore (43 percent), as did Catholics, but more narrowly (49 percent to 47 percent); while Jews were emphatically for Gore (79 percent) over Bush (19 percent). If there's a vast right-wing religious conspiracy afoot, it's extremely well camouflaged. The truth is that it's a mythological beast, a whipping boy of liberals who love to pick fights with people who don't fight back.

President Bush

"In the two years since Sept. 11, 2001, the view of the United States as a victim of terrorism that deserved the world's sympathy and support has given way to a widespread vision of America as an imperial power that has defied world opinion through unjustified and unilateral use of military force. . . . To some degree, the resentment is centered on the person of President Bush, who is seen by many of those interviewed, at best, as an ineffective spokesman for American interests and, at worst, as a gunslinging cowboy knocking over international treaties and bent on controlling the world's oil, if not the entire world."
— **Richard Bernstein,** *The New York Times,* September 11, 2003

"We have a President who stole the presidency through family ties, arrogance, and intimidation, employing Republican operatives to

exercise the tactics of voter fraud by disenfranchising thousands of blacks, elderly Jews, and other minorities."
— **Barbra Streisand**, April 3, 2001

"I despise him [President George W. Bush]. I despise his administration and everything they stand for. . . . To my mind the election was stolen by George Bush, and we have been suffering ever since under this man's leadership. . . . I think this latest thing with Iraq is absolute madness, and I'm stunned that there is not opposition on a much more global scale to what he's talking about. . . . There has to be a movement now to really oppose what he is proposing because it's unconstitutional, it's immoral, and basically illegal. . . . It is an embarrassing time to be an American. It really is. It's humiliating."
— **Jessica Lange**, May 19, 2003

"What happened to the compassion that was supposed to go with Bush's conservatism? The campaign prepared us for some of this—candidate Bush made plain his intention to drill in the Arctic wildlife refuge, not a bad political calculus given America's preference for SUVs over caribou. But no one thought his team would choose slaughterhouses over schoolchildren, even if only for a day. What connects these decisions is a preference for folks he knows: his oil-field buddies (mirrors of himself), corporate executives and captains of industry, from the Halliburton honcho to the Terminix franchisee."
—**Margaret Carlson,** *Time,* April 16, 2001

"The real terrorist threats are George W. Bush and his band of brown-shirted thugs."
— **Sandra Bernhard**, February 25, 2002

"I hate President George W. Bush. . . I hate the way he walks. . .
I hate the way he talks. . . And, while most people who meet
Bush claim to like him, I suspect that, if I got to know
him personally, I would hate him even more."
— **Jonathan Chait,** *The New Republic*, September 9, 2003

Before we even begin with the truth of Mr. George W. Bush, let's note something fascinating in these quotes and the ones throughout this book. An astonishing number of them come from persons in or from New York, a national center of tension and anger. Most of the rest come from Southern California, another place filled with angry people. Let's also note that what we see on display in these quotes is a level of anger so breathtaking that it is almost a self-diagnostic tool of mental unwellness all by itself, often from people with a history of mental illness. But we'll get to that later.

It's often implied in the media that President Bush is stupid. This is a hoax. His verbal SAT score of 566 in the mid-1960s translates into a score of 632 today, after the "dumbing down" of the SATs in 1994. That puts him at the 91st percentile of verbal intelligence, the best estimate of overall IQ. According to the College Board, because of the statistical uncertainties inherent in these measurements, a person's post-1994 SAT verbal score would have to be above 692 to demonstrate that he had better verbal skills than those of our President. George W. Bush's math score on the SAT was 640, equivalent to a score of 648 today. If your post-1994 math SAT was higher than 708, you can tell all your friends that you have better math skills than Mr. Bush. Be our guest.

President Bush graduated from Yale University. He wasn't first in his class, but he was smart enough to earn a degree from one of the most challenging schools in the world. And unlike Senator Ted Kennedy, Mr. Bush didn't hire anyone to take his exams or write his term papers for him. Second, he graduated from Harvard Business School, where you don't graduate unless you pass your tests and turn in your papers. Who was the last President who had an earned, not honorary, degree from an Ivy League college and an Ivy League graduate school? That would be Franklin D. Roosevelt, who went to Harvard University and Columbia Law School (both Bush and Roosevelt came from prestigious East Coast families with Ivy League pedigrees). No one has recently called Roosevelt a dummy.

After school, among many other achievements, Bush learned to pilot a jet fighter—hardly a job for the slow-witted. After that, he became a success in the major-league baseball business. Sure, he used his connections to get the gig—but who on earth doesn't? How many children, brothers, or cousins of Presidents screw up terribly while making use of connections? Bush used his skillfully and lawfully, without hurting anyone, and became a multimillionaire.

Then there's the matter of his being a wildly popular governor of the second-largest state in the nation by population and area, and then acing out far more experienced hands to become the GOP nominee. Finally, Bush ran a campaign that defeated the incumbent vice president of a popular President during a period of prosperity and peace to become President of the United States of America. Not a terrible résumé, to be sure.

Any critic can make fun of the guy who's down in the arena doing things. But when that guy makes great things happen for himself and achieves an astonishing level of success, how can we call him anything but smart? There have been 43 Presidents, and almost all had children—yet only two of those kids got to be President (the other was John Quincy Adams back in 1825). It's not automatic; Bush made it happen. You can open the tabloids any day of the week and read of people born to vastly greater privilege than President Bush who have made less than nothing of their lives.

Of course, if having a high IQ all by itself made a person a great President, then we'd be carving Richard Nixon's face into Mount Rushmore by now. Instead, what's wanted (but not always delivered) is a certain quality of *character* or *leadership* that's hard to define . . . but the American people know it when they see it. Remember how the country breathed a collective sigh of relief after 9/11 when it reflected that it hadn't elected Al Gore? That's because Bush has these qualities to spare. A class-mate of Bush's at Yale recalls how a bunch of students in the dorm were sitting around one night cutting down a kid who wasn't there. No doubt some of us might have been tempted to join them, if only to fit in and be liked. Bush didn't; instead, he told his pals that the kid had had a tough life and that they should knock it off. That's a future President talking, a person of character.

Consider this story about an encounter with a man of faith at church in the winter of 2004:

> I'm at the 8:00 A.M. service at my church, St. John's at Lafayette Square, across from the White House. Much of the service was uneventful—nice, but uneventful—until it comes to the part of the service when the priest says, "Greet one another in the name of the Lord." I turn to my right to exchange the peace with my friend, who was on the other end of my pew. I then shake hands with the person in front of me, and turn around to say hello to the person behind me.
>
> The person behind me was our 43rd President, George W. Bush. I am not kidding. A small crowd was forming around him, and not wanting to delay the church service or bother him by waiting to shake his hand, I turned back around and sat down and talked to Amy. About 30 seconds later I felt a

hand on my left shoulder and turn around to see President Bush with his hand extended.

"Peace of the Lord," he said, and held my hand with both of his.

"Peace of the Lord," I replied, and held both his hands and smiled at him.

I turned back around and was remarkably calm about the fact that the most powerful person in the world was sitting two feet behind me. I could hear him flipping through his bulletin as the priest made the announcements. I loved the idea of him thinking, *Oh, there's a covered dish next Sunday.*

We perched, and when I stood up to go to the communion rail, he got up and walked down the aisle behind me. We passed a little old lady who said, "Mr. President, I pray for you every day." To which he said, "That's a very special gift. Thank you so much." We got to the communion rail and there were two spaces, one in front of us and one around the side of the altar. We both surmised for ten seconds, and then I started off around the corner. He stopped me and whispered, "No, no. I'll go around," and motioned for me to take the closer spot. The only exception made in the entire service was that the President was allowed to leave first and then the rest of the congregation followed.

With all sincerity, and partisanship aside, I tell you: This is a special man! There is a peace and Godliness about him. It radiates from him. It is the only reason that I was able to remain calm. It was more than the adrenaline I've felt when I've met other famous people. A goodness flows through this man. He has more than my vote in November. He has my respect, my prayers, and my gratitude. Whatever your political affiliation, and whether or not you agree with his decisions, you should take comfort in the fact that, despite recent press attacks—this is a man of integrity who makes decisions because he believes they are right, not popular. He makes these decisions with a heavy heart and through prayer.

I don't mean to go on and on, but I truly believe this was a blessing from God that should be passed on.

Does this sound like the kind of man you'd be afraid to have leading the nation, or the kind of man you'd be grateful to have leading the nation in time of crisis? Does this sound like the kind of man you can fear or the kind you can trust? We all want as President a man we would want as a friend—in 2000, we were lucky to get one.

★★★ ★★★

Chapter

The Radical Left

L et's pause and review what we've discovered thus far:

- The Left claims that the U.S. economy is an engine
  of social oppression. It is, in fact, a miracle of prosperity creation.

- The Left claims that globalization is destroying the
  planet. Yet it's actually saving the world's poor from
  the misery, disease, illiteracy, and starvation that
  have always been their lot.

- The Left claims that the United States military is a
  crushing presence around the world. In fact, the
  American people, acting through their military,
  have twice saved the world from totalitarianism,
  while asking nothing in return; and at this very
  moment, that military is saving us from the menace of Islamic fundamentalism.

- The Left claims that America is a racist and sexist society, regardless of the fact that the United States fought a bloody war to end slavery. In recent years, it has promoted equality on a scale and with an alacrity that are without historical precedent.

- The Left claims that we're destroying the environment, and that some international body controlled by them needs to take control lest some disaster befall. In fact, the U.S. has made tremendous strides toward pollution abatement and environmental salvation while the real pollution problems come from Asia and South America.

- The Left, on occasion, abuses the social sciences to hurl spitballs at conservatives while hiding behind a fig leaf of scientific objectivity. In fact, some of their research looks a lot more like politically motivated left-wing propaganda.

Since what the Left perceives is egregiously at odds with the facts, this poses the question: What is the genesis of this misperception of reality?

Ignorance Is Bliss?

Undeniably, ignorance must be counted as one of the causes of liberal bias. The educational system of this country has collapsed to such an extent that Americans, especially but by no means exclusively young Americans, simply have no idea of what the rest of the world is like and what history is. When the *United States History Standards* mention George Washington once and the Ku Klux Klan 19 times, we see the scope of the problem. Many, if not most, colleges no longer require that students take a course in American history as a prerequisite for graduation. Even if they did take such a course, considering who our university teachers are and what their biases are, it's questionable what these students would learn.

Many people today have no idea that the rest of the world is far behind the United States in terms of prosperity, legal protection of the citizenry, career and educational opportunities, and racial openness. In the minds of these ignorant men, women, and children, outside the U.S. exists a golden land where there's no discrimination, and peace and plenty reign under coconut palms without labor or strife. Obviously, if folks sincerely believed that life is better outside of America, then they'd have good reason to be angered by conditions here at home. Why shouldn't the U.S. be as prosperous, open, or safe as Denmark, Belarus, or Zimbabwe? For these people, some measure of education might be helpful, but there's a saying here that applies: "None are so blind as those who will not see."

Then again, for some haters of America, the comparison is instead made with a mythical Eden that existed many years ago. According to these critics, until America stomped the world with her size-13 boots made for walking, Earth was a preindustrial paradise where avarice and poverty were unknown. Now if people really believed in this golden age, then of course they'd be bound to feel terrible about the state of our country, with its crime, crowding, pollution, and unemployment. In other words, they might simply be unaware that the world that existed before massive industrialization, and especially before the postwar era of mass prosperity, was a far worse and sadder place than the one we take for granted today. Before the mid-20th century in the Western world, poverty and oppression really were the constants of human life. Possibly some reading of history would help here as well, although the same warning about willful ignorance does apply.

The Mind-set Behind Hating America

There are many left-wingers whose hatred of America doesn't rest on ignorance. Naturally, we don't wish to tar all liberals with this brush; in fact, we're fans of many liberals and Democrats. But we can't help but notice that there's a certain constellation of traits that seems to go hand-in-hand with a generalized hatred of this country.

While there are many studies on the so-called conservative personality, there's almost nothing written on the psychology of liberals. Freud's essay on Woodrow Wilson would certainly be an exception, but his study is limited to a single man, not a type. Is it possible that the Marxist and left-wing bias in the field of psychology (which presently gives us such scientific journals as *Cannabis Therapeutics, Journal of Lesbian Studies, Feminist Family Therapy, Journal of Gay and Lesbian Issues in Education,* and *Journal of Bisexuality*) has caused these scientists of the mind, perhaps by some unconscious defense mechanism, to look for the mote in others' eyes, instead of the beam in their own? Having acknowledged this vacuum in the psychological literature, no doubt psychologists will be eager to correct the imbalance. (That's a joke, in case you wondered.)

We don't deny that psychological predispositions can underlie political belief. Psychological predispositions, we assume, are behind almost any kind of belief. It certainly applies in law. The whole theory of legal realism, developed mostly at Yale but also at Harvard and Columbia, by Harold Lasswell, Myres McDougall, and Karl Llewellyn, says that judges make up their minds about cases based on their own personal views and prejudices, and then clothe their decisions with "precedents" and "statutes" to make it look as if they are impartially reading some "brooding omnipresence in the sky" called law.

Because in any important legal case at the appellate level, there will be ample precedent on both sides of the issue, and judges can always find some reason to apply some bits of it to rationalize their own prejudices, some other factors have to be at work, and these are the personal predilections of the judges. In other words, the judges make up their minds about a case because they like the plaintiff's legs, they go to the same country club as the defendant, or relate to something similar that happened to them once in college, and then they make up a lot of interesting reasons for why they reach their decisions.

Legal realism was further refined by Alex Bickel and then Robert Bork (although they might not have called it that), who said that if judges could find even the faintest shred or shadow of a precedent to "legitimize" their own prejudices, they would do so and act as if they were reaching a conclusion any sane and learned Justice would reach. The great examples of this are the abortion decisions in which the court found a right of privacy that covered the right to murder a baby, and claimed that there were "penumbras" and "emanations" from the Fourth and Fourteenth Amendments to legitimize this right to murder, when really there was no such thing.

By the same token then, *political* realism says that people in a free society make up their minds about an issue based on whether or not they hate their fathers and mothers, whether or not they're oriented toward the same sex, whether or not they feel sexually confident, and a million other psychological reasons—and then they make up a rationale based on public policy to justify whatever it is they're doing. We offer this as a theory as to why the radical Left behaves as it does (and we want a Nobel Prize for it right this second!).

The Lure of Socialism and Control

The reason socialism, or something like it, will never die is because the socialist ideology satisfies some of our most potent psychological needs: power, control, significance in life, and so on. Karl Marx, in the most sweeping political formulation since "All men are created equal," said, "All history is the history of class struggle." It was a beguiling hypothesis, but it's since fallen flat on its face. Working people don't want to annihilate the middle class; instead, they want to be a *part* of the middle class and then the upper class—and many do just that in America.

Class analysis of history has proved useful, however, as a means of providing well-paid work and power to intellectuals, who are the best and most brutal at class analysis. This covers up otherwise bizarre usurpations of authority by people who want to control their fellow human beings. It's natural and normal, and we assume all people do it—that is, use moral principles to rationalize their own desires and wishes. But when certain people use moral rationales to do damage to the world around them because of their own rage, frustration, and need for control, terrible harm can be (and is) done. History is largely about the behavior of very capable mentally ill people as they come into contact with the larger world beyond their imagination.

Who was Napoleon Bonaparte but a compulsive paranoid, needing to subjugate as much of the world as possible so that he could impose on it the minutely detailed regulations he made up out of his head? He lost more than 500,000 men in Russia alone—a high price for extending the French "enlightenment" to the world—yet Napoleon is regarded as a hero. Similarly, what was World War I except the work of a megalomaniac Kaiser confronting a resolute allied power? What was World War II except the machinations of several paranoid maniacs—Hitler,

Himmler, Goebbels, Mussolini, and the Japanese military elite—venting their problems on the world in the guise of various ideologies of race and socialism? What is the history of Red Bolshevism but a struggle for power and control by some horribly psychotic obsessive-compulsives who used the rhetoric of class struggle, but could have just as easily used the Protocols of the Learned Elders of Zion to achieve their personal ends and meet their psychological needs?

When maniac controllers establish behavioral systems to keep people from doing what they want, they don't act alone. Bolshevism, for instance, worked for as long as it did because there were a great many other people in Russia besides Stalin, Beria, and Vishinsky who liked to boss people around, locked in an unhealthy symbiosis with still others who liked being bossed around. Likewise, in Hitler's Germany, an authoritarian system provided many openings for commissars, planners, and ministers of fear.

These behavioral systems also solve a problem for people whose anxieties about how they should behave on a daily basis can be resolved by being ordered about. Think of the mobs of delirious Austrians and Sudeten Germans welcoming der Führer, the worshipful crowds shouting "Perón!" and the old Communists in Russia who even now lament the fall of socialism in their country. Socialism serves the psychological needs of certain human beings, just as political orders built on the blueprints of Jefferson and Madison appeal to those of us who like freedom.

It's our contention that people who choose freedom are generally more psychologically mature than those who seek to control or be controlled; and they have internalized images of "father" and "mother" that are healthier. Being capable of self-regulation and self-government, they're not looking for external rules and regulations handed down from a domineering state to quell the monsters within.

Despite statism's grim history, there are still a lot of people in the United States demanding strict government regulation of society, lest they be unbearably threatened by successes and liberties of their fellow citizens. Radical feminists, often very unhappy people, rail against the differentiations of nature and the occupational and domestic choices of their neighbors. Atheists insist that no one ever be allowed to worship in school. Environmentalists find an ecological justification for even the most minute controls, in a manipulative impulse that places exacting limitations on society and individuals.

Again, even those who have some legitimate concerns use a wildly inflated version of them to acquire power over others and—very important—over themselves. Health care is another moral issue that allows people to control other people. The architects of the Clinton health-care plan—who may be back in town one day soon—would have made it a crime punishable by prison to go to your own doctor if a cheaper one were available. Controllers remain a formidable presence, always ready to step in when given the slightest opening.

A certain kind of unhappy human spirit craves to command and to be commanded. The great genius of Marxism new and old is that it responds cunningly to that need while clothing it in glittering moral garments. Marxism says, "We're instituting a system of rigid controls solely for the sake of the little guy, those who labor, and the poor. Only selfish oppressors will resist giving up their freedoms for this cause." For absolute domination that crosses over lines of sex, class, and religion, few movements can match its appeal, both before (in its discredited classic form) and now (in its new "Marxist lite" incarnations). In fact, radical feminism, atheism, and environmentalism are all offshoots: "Sexual equality" must be preceded by economic equality in a workers' society; radical environmental protection requires keeping the resources of the earth for "the people" rather than private owners; and so forth. Socialism is the biggest umbrella available to control people, a tent large enough to encompass almost any cause underneath.

Peace demonstrators are often depressed and feel insignificant and are furiously, violently angry (just look at their faces). Joining a movement addresses all of these concerns: It gives people public visibility and allows them a forum to express their rage and homicidal urges (such as calling for death to Bush and comparing him with Hitler), while at the same time allowing them to publicly express their moral superiority. More than peace, however, demonstrators' real goal might well be to jam the gears of the father figure, George W. Bush, and the United States, and to thereby give their otherwise depressed lives some meaning. Gun-control demonstrators are an even clearer case in point: In the guise of calling for gun regulations, these people really can fight their own murderous urges to kill by projecting their disowned feelings onto gun owners and then emasculating them.

Of course, pro-Bush and pro-defense people also feel insecurities, but they want to address them by an appeal to their symbolic Daddy (the President) and symbolic male authority figures (such as the military). This is a far more direct and less tortured path to working out their inner feelings, which is why pro-defense forces look quite calm and peaceful, while anti-war forces look tortured and crazy.

The Psychology of the Left

We note the following features of leftist complaint. And again, we don't presume to say that all on the Left are ill, unhappy, or deficient psychologically. Many of them are fine people with good points to make. And no doubt many crazy ones found other routes to get wherever they are. But as for some of them . . .

1. The Left wants someone to make them powerful. They want the state to give them the power to take money away from undeserving people and corporations and then give it to others who are poor. They want the state to guarantee certain racial, gender, and environmental outcomes, thus reshaping the world into the way they want it to be. And they want to be in charge of the process(es).

2. The Left wants control. They want to decide the allocation of resources, instead of living with the mess made by capitalism and the open market, with its arbitrary and unfair winners and losers.

3. The Left wants attention. They want admiration for their brilliance and for their boundless compassion toward all forms of life.

4. The Left is angry—they're full of rage at the way things are and the unfairness of the status quo; and they talk in harsh, uncompromising terms against the injustice they see everywhere around them.

5. The Left wants to "make love, not war." They want to talk, work through diplomatic channels, and use words instead of weapons. They're willing to take up arms only when every other option has been completely exhausted. Even here, they don't want to fight without clear goals, methods, and definitive outcomes in mind, so they know in advance

how the battle will turn out. On the other hand, when leftist dictators do take up arms, they do so with a violence and breadth of rage that makes capitalists seem like pacifists. And the American left applauds or looks the other way.

Now, what are the corresponding psychological states that give rise to these attitudes?

1. When we feel a need for power, it's because we feel *powerless*.

2. When we feel a need for control, it's because we feel *out of control*.

3. When we want attention and admiration, it's because we feel *overlooked* and *neglected*.

4. When we feel rage, it's because we're *fearful* and *envious*.

5. When we're reluctant to fight, it's because we feel *vulnerable*, or because we feel *grandiose* and omnipotent and fear that our power will destroy everything... or secretly want our power to destroy everything.

These characteristics, taken together, describe the characteristic anomalies of what might be called "the infantile personality." The image comes to mind of a powerless little baby who needs someone to take charge, demanding that its primary narcissism be fueled with endless attention and admiration, lashing out and flailing with delusions of omnipotence that mask an underlying fear of impotence.

Now, what might be the origin of this reluctance to grow up? Again, we offer a few speculations as guides for future research. (And again, these are speculations, hypotheses but by no means conclusions.)

In part, we believe this attitude has to do with a failure to integrate the image of the father into the psyche. The metaphor is apt whether or not a causal connection is ever proved. This deficiency might appear, for example, when the father is absent, either physically or emotionally. Alternatively, the father himself may be a weak or immature personality who fails to leave an imprint. Either way, this lack of integration leads to a person feeling out of control, and to a possible eventual search for the state to provide what he or she failed to find in the family. It also leads to a hatred for the weak or absent father (and fear of the father, as well as of one's own feelings of hatred for the father), coupled with a deep unconscious longing for a real father.

This is why left-wing regimes are best run by totalitarian figures like Stalin or Saddam (the return of the hated but longed-for father), but weaker, fatherlike Presidents such as Bush or Nixon are despised. The best compromise is the immature boy-President: the Kennedy or Clinton type favored by American liberals. But a boyish President like Bush who has a successfully internalized father is hated with special gusto, born of a bottomless psychological envy. (And again, we emphasize that these are hypotheses only.)

A second possible factor in the development of the anti-American type might be the presence of the cold mother. This is the woman who, while perfunctorily performing the quotidian demands of motherhood, does so with thinly veiled hostility and resentment. Psychologically, she resembles nothing so much as the surrogate mothers made of wire and terry cloth used in the classic experiments Harry Harlow performed on some unfortunate rhesus monkeys in the 1950s. The life stance is an angry demand for restitution for the treatment suffered at her hands. The child, feeling abandoned and aware that its emotional needs are unmet, fantasizes about an idealized, soft, warm, big-bosomed, all-loving, and providing mother. When this isn't found in the family, it's eventually looked for from the state—a big government to make everything all right with a paradise of plenty for the "downtrodden" with whom the liberal identifies (even from a penthouse on the Upper West Side).

Under the pretense of comparing current social conditions to some objective template, the real world is always held up against the Eden of the unconscious fantasized perfect mother and found wanting. In the face of an internalized sense of emptiness and worthlessness, no measures can ever be enough.

Left-Wing "Compassion"

As adults, such individuals may make some show of being outwardly compassionate, but they're really cold inside, black holes of unmet emotional need. The bogus compassion that's a hallmark of the Left has its roots in a classic childhood role reversal. The needy, crazy, or angry mother turns the child into a psychological parent for herself—that is, the physical child is conscripted into becoming the mother's psychological parent, taking care of the resentful mom for emotional survival. When this child grows up, the ostensible compassion (in some but by no means all cases) masks a codependent search for someone to take care of him or her. Meanwhile, playing the "compassion" card provides the secondary gain of trumping all other arguments with the inherent moral superiority of the liberal. Thus, today even ex-Communists are considered good guys because of their professed deep compassion for humanity, while ex-Fascists and ex-Klansmen have difficulty scaring up the best dinner-party invitations. Who cares if Stalin murdered 50,000,000 people? At least his heart was in the right place.

In truth, do-gooding was never the point, which is perhaps why so few left-wing schemes, from the Communist revolutions to the New Deal to the Great Society, have amounted to anything worthwhile. As Ayn Rand suggested and many others have noted, compassion is just the camouflage under which the Left endeavors to seize power. Gustave Le Bon described socialists this way in his pre-Freudian *The Psychology of Socialism* (1899):

> Social failures, misunderstood geniuses, lawyers without clients, writers without readers, doctors without patients, professors ill-paid, graduates without employment, clerks whose employers disdain them for their insufficiency, puffed-up university instructors—these are the natural adepts of Socialism. In reality they care little for doctrines. Their dream is to create by violent means a society in which they will be the masters. Their cry of equality does not prevent them from having an intense scorn of the rabble who have not, as they have, learned out of books.

There's no deep desire for oneness with the masses here. Equality is fine for other people, so long as we're in charge.

★★★ ★★★

Chapter

The Special Case
of Hollywood

"When I see an American flag flying, it's a joke."
— Robert Altman, January 21, 2002

*"I not only think that they [U.S. leaders] are misguided, but
I think they know exactly what they are doing, and I think
that they are men who are possessed of evil."*
— Harry Belafonte, April 4, 2003

"We can't beat anyone anymore."
— George Clooney, February 23, 2003

*"We have a President for whom English is a second
language. He's like 'We have to get rid of dictators,' but he's
pretty much one himself."*
— Robin Williams, March 31, 2003

"I think war is based in greed and there are huge karmic retributions that will follow. I think war is never the answer to solving any problems. The best way to solve problems is to not have enemies."
— **Sheryl Crow,** January 13, 2003

"I think the U.S. is terrifying, and it saddens me."
— **Tom Cruise,** June 27, 2002

"I don't know if a country [America] where the people are so ignorant of reality and of history, if you can call that a free world."
— **Jane Fonda,** April 8, 2003

"In a situation like this, of course you identify with everyone who's suffering. [But we must also think about] the terrorists who are creating such horrible future lives for themselves because of the negativity of this karma. It's all of our jobs to keep our minds as expansive as possible. If you can see [the terrorists] as a relative who's dangerously sick, and we have to give them medicine . . . the medicine is love and compassion—there's nothing better."
— **Richard Gere,** October 9, 2001

"Melt their weapons, melt their hearts, melt their anger with love."
— **Shirley MacLaine,** October 8, 2001

"I remember when I was a kid, you know, this whole Cold War thing. They had us scared of the Russians. 'The Russians, the Russians, the Russians.' So it's almost like what's real and what's not?"
— **Queen Latifah,** February 12, 2003

Almost every middle-aged American can easily recall the images of Hollywood pitching in to fight World War II: Jimmy Stewart quitting acting to fly bombers (as did Clark Gable); the entire town cranking out movies glorifying America and its war effort, endlessly encouraging the nation in its life-and-death struggle against the Nazis and the Japanese. Think of *Guadalcanal Diary* and *Thirty Seconds Over Tokyo;* think of the cavalcades of stars touring the armed forces throughout the world—Bob Hope, Esther Williams, and all the other big names doing what they could to win the war.

Today, what Hollywood is saying about the struggle between the humane, decent values of this nation and the bloodthirsty rage of the Muslim extremist terrorists is vastly different from the patriotic sentiments of yesteryear. It's enough to make a grown man or woman weep.

Hollywood's Anger

So what happened to change Hollywood's views about America so dramatically? Where did all this anger, this loathing of the country that made them demigods, come from? Why, in other words, do so many (but by no means all) people in Hollywood hold the standard world view of a left-wing college student from the Bronx in 1937 or a blissed-out flower child from Haight-Ashbury in 1968? Where did the Hollywood "beautiful people's" devout love of their country go?

Put another way, perhaps never before in history have a people so wildly privileged in a nation felt such hostility and/or confusion toward it. But why? Why does America, which has been so wildly, unbelievably good to the people of Hollywood—at least the power people of Hollywood—inspire, terrify, and bewilder them?

Partly, it has to do with social competition. Those on Hollywood's top rung have so much power, so much money, and so many acolytes kissing their behinds that they simply can't believe that there are entire sections of the country who have even more political and economic power than they do. They're furiously angry about it, like small children who can't believe that anybody else could share their parents' attention. The fact that some of those other "haves" are often Republicans is just maddeningly frustrating to people so accustomed to getting their own way.

Yet, if Hollywood realizes that it doesn't have a monopoly on power in the United States (and that fact drives them crazy), then who does have it, as far as the town is concerned? Not the politicians. As Marx pointed out, politicians are just the lackeys, lickspittles, and long-tongued running dogs of the exploiting class. And the people of Hollywood may hate the politicians who aren't under their control, sitting up and begging them for money, but they "know" the truth about where power resides in this world. No, to the infantile Marxists of Hollywood, the real power in the society belongs to the big businessmen, the puppeteers who pull the politicians' strings.

As perfectly revealed in Oliver Stone's *Nixon*, there is supposedly a shadowy conspiracy of rich industrialists, Wall Street financiers, and Texas oilmen who control the nation, especially via the Republican party. "Monopoly" capital, as the last and most potent antagonist of the working classes according to Marx, is by definition evil. The multimillionaire artistes of Hollywood, allies of the proletarian vanguard, are the heroic enemies of those fascistic exploiters (who happen to employ the entire Bush administration as lackeys, by the way).

There's a great book on this subject called *Hollywood Party* by Kenneth Lloyd Billingsley, but to put it simply, Marxism—as a basic, easy-to-grasp way of pretending to be moral while wielding a big, gold-plated stick—attached itself like a leech to Hollywood in the 1930s and really never let go. It became the lay religion of the town, the groupthink *sine qua non* of membership in certain (but by no means all) Hollywood inside circles. And naturally, as Marxists, certain Hollywood powers have to hate Bush—and they do—and hate his war effort against terrorism.

(Again, we're talking here about the most vocal and angry examples. There are many fine men and women in this town, in fact, who quietly and doggedly support and love this country and would sacrifice anything for it. Some of them are extremely left wing in many of their political views, but this doesn't keep them from being courageous, sensible people. Neither the GOP in Hollywood, small as it is, nor the GOP anywhere, large as it is, has a monopoly on truth and decency. Alas, the most angry and anti-American of the powers in Hollywood get most of the ink—the quiet, hardworking people are, well, quiet.)

Cheated in L.A.

While the commonplace Hollywood dislike of business and the American government (which is seen as merely the executive committee of the ruling monopolist class) has a Marxist component, there is something even more basically human at work here: The Hollywood pooh-bahs' feeling that they've personally been cheated. Feeling persecuted is a way of life in this town. It works something like this: Hollywood writers, as an important example (they're a disproportionately, ideologically powerful group because they're the "intellectuals" of the town), feel cheated if they make $20,000 per week, because they always know someone whom they hate who makes $50,000 a week; and the ones who make 50 thou a week know someone who makes 100K a week—the ladder of envy goes up to the sky. Every writer seems to have tales of studio rip-offs and network indifference that make their blood boil.

Unlike college professors, Hollywood scribes have direct experience with business, and they feel cheated. They all wrote scripts just like *The Lord of the Rings* that somehow got ripped off. They all had ideas for shows like *Seinfeld,* only better, that never got made. They were all promised profit participations, which they never received. So, no matter how rich they are, and they can be *very* rich, they always feel victimized. (No matter that, as despised as they are in Hollywood, the writers set the "moral" tone here—just because they're almost the only ones who give any thought to anything besides how they look. Plus, they have the raw power of writing what appears on the screen.)

Regardless of the power they do enjoy, Hollywood writers also feel envious of the businesspeople they meet. Usually studio executives, these "suits" often make more money, have more power, and (sometimes) enjoy more job security. So do agents. Writers are therefore envious of the powerful studio or network executives or agents in their midst, with their nicer cars, bigger houses, and trophy wives, and their power to hire and fire the writers. The executives aren't eaten up by the self-loathing that the Hollywood writer feels—so the writer channels this anger by depicting businesspeople as thugs, murderers, assassins, and polluters.

Writers then direct their anger against the father figure, the lackey of the business class, the eternal stranger—the GOP President. If that President is waging a war, then the war must be unjust. If that President is saying that he's trying to preserve America, then he must be lying—and he must be out to get the Hollywood powers that be. Why? Because if they don't have a powerful enemy who can harm them, how can they be true heroes? A hero has to have jeopardy, as any screenwriter knows. A hero has to have enemies more powerful than he is, or else he isn't much of a hero when he wins. Bush is that enemy. Therefore, the U.S., which dares to elect people like Bush, has to be the enemy as well.

(And we don't even have time to go into how America sheltered and nurtured the Klan—which many in Hollywood believe runs the country once you get east of Palm Springs and west of Jersey City, and how America has whole towns that don't even serve Perrier at their restaurants.)

To an earlier generation of Hollywood stars, many of whom had some actual experience with the country east of Palm Springs, America was a glorious, gilded place. But to the men and women of Hollywood today, many of whom are from big cities or from Hollywood itself for most of their lives, America is as strange and frightening—except as a source of ratings and ticket sales—as Mars might be. How can it be anything but terrifying if it elects Republicans in large numbers and drives American-made cars?

Hollywood feels estranged from America, deeply misunderstands America, and might even envy America (at least a little bit) for its imagined peace of mind. Plus, it hates and fears big business, which it imagines runs America. Small wonder then that Hollywood (and again, we don't mean all of Hollywood— we especially don't mean the teamsters, gaffers, sound people, and makeup artists whose names no one knows, yet who do all of the heavy lifting) turns its anger against America and her projects, such as saving the world from terrorism. It would be different if the 9/11 terrorists had bombed Gucci or the yoga instructors or Pilates teachers, but the terrorists didn't do that— they targeted Wall Street and the Pentagon, and that makes a big difference. What the terrorists did is almost understandable to some of the most benighted minds here. It all comes under the heading of "biting the hand that feeds you" . . . but then so much of what this book is about comes under the same heading.

The bitter tragedy here is that Hollywood is desperately needed right now to rally the nation, to make us feel proud of ourselves, and to encourage us in the global struggle against the terrorists and their allies. Sadly, too much of the star network that used to be out there selling savings bonds is now selling self-loathing and self-reproach—and, above all, an ugly doubt about whether a kind, humane society like ours is really any better than one run by people in caves in Afghanistan who murder children and laugh about it, and think that they're doing God's will.

★★★ ★★★

Envy

E nvy is the emotional nuclear-power generator that fuels every sort of evil on Earth. It's not an accident that this emotion is mentioned in the Bible in such negative terms on so many occasions. It's also the fuel that powers a great deal of the anti-Americanism found at home and abroad.

What Envy Can Spawn

Envy works in a fairly simple way. There are a lot of people who are jealous of the success of the planet's movers and shakers, along with the groups, religions, ethnicities, and nations of the world who have made it. Since there are ethical injunctions against their saying and feeling, "Hey, I'm jealous of those more successful than I am. They've got some special something I want. I can't figure out how to get it by any legitimate means, so I think I'll steal it," they say, "It's not that I'm jealous. It's that the entrepreneur is exploiting the workers." Or, "America is a vicious Philistine exploiter that needs to be restrained for the good of the workers." Or, "The Jews are a clique that tricks, exploits, and steals. Let's kill them and take what they have for the greater good of the Aryan race." But it's all the same. It's all envy.

Those who have to cloak their envy and their wish to control in moral terms such as helping the poor, the children, the workers, *Das Reich,* or trees are dangerous. Of course there are genuinely great causes involving poor people, workers, and the environment that can be helped by decent people without crazy psychological agendas. But the sick and envious are weak, frightened people who can be led to unspeakable evil, especially when they cloak their jealousy in moral garments.

Envy wrapped in fake morality tells people that it's all right to perpetrate horrific acts upon others just because the victims were harder working, more industrious, or just luckier; and it rationalizes the class conflict that leads to mass murders. For example, the most sinister ideologist of all time, Karl Marx, was a poor member of a wealthy German-Jewish family. His envy of his rich, capitalist cousins was unbridled—and he rationalized it in great, stupefying detail as a critique of the whole capitalist system called *Das Kapital.*

In a shorter version, *The Communist Manifesto,* he electrified millions and began the entire collectivist movement that turned much of the earth into a slaughterhouse. All this sprang from one very sick, very brilliant man's jealousy of his very rich capitalist Jewish uncles and cousins. (We're indebted to Paul Johnson for this insight.) The Communists then used envy as a basic tool to start the Lenin–Stalin dictatorship that eventually ate up the lives of tens of millions of every social class. The Nazis also used envy of the Jews to start the Holocaust. In modern east-central Africa, envy between Hutu and Tutsi led to some of the worst butchery ever seen. Likewise, envy cloaked in moral garments in Cambodia, China, and Vietnam killed millions of totally innocent people. The Southern Hemisphere is still scarred from its effects in South America and Cuba, while the greatest danger to man's survival right now is the Islamofascist movement that menaces the globe.

Envy is a force like racism that, once started, is very difficult to stop and can be used to justify anything. Does anyone seriously doubt that jealousy of our Western way of life was the principal motivation behind the attacks on 9/11? Who better to be envious of than a society of people who have more power than you, who have more money than you, and who have better lives than you? When we humans envy a class of people, all too often we hate them. If we can then say that our hatred is a moral, cleansing sentiment, we can allow it to push us to do any evil.

A small world example: economists Andrew Oswald and Daniel Zizzo were surprised by their own findings about envy in economics. They devised a simple experiment where they gave cash unequally to students, telling them about the inequitable distribution of wealth among them. Then they gave each student the option of anonymously burning another student's money, with the proviso that in the process, each would also have to burn some of his or her own. The rational response is not to burn any money, since you'd have to destroy your own property in the process. Instead, 62 percent of students burned their fellow classmates' money, even at a high cost to themselves. It was far more important to hurt those who were better off than to do better themselves. On a large scale, this kind of attitude can lead to suicide bombing; on a smaller scale, it can lead to more minor mischief, but mischief all the same.

The tragedies of Communism, Fascism, and ethnic mass murder all have to do with envy in a big way. The rage that many on the Left feel toward successful people of all stripes—and often just plain different people who happen to be Republicans or conservatives—shares this basis in a much smaller way. But this anger in America today based on envy has a particularly unfortunate set of consequences: It tends to attack the U.S. as a nation in an attempt to delegitimize the country. In other words, the envious say that their failure comes not from themselves, but because the cards are stacked against them by an illegitimate nation and system (that is, a racist, oppressive, gender-biased, environmentally destructive system, as we've previously mentioned). If the charge that the United States is an evil system is made often enough, it gets to be believed by many people—and this kind of attitude is extremely dangerous in a time of prolonged war.

As motive for the intense anger that many on the Left feel toward our nation, let's turn to a special and especially ugly form of envy: Phariseeism.

★★★ ★★★

Phariseeism

A basic reason for criticism of the United States and our way of life might be deemed *Phariseeism*. This could be described in a number of ways—and we'll do just that—but one simple way of expressing it would be that the critic (or the Pharisee) is better, holier, and more morally upright than you because he drives an old Volvo (always a foreign car, by the way), while you drive a new Chevy Suburban. Or, to put it in a way that a dictionary writer might like better, Phariseeism is the belief that a man or woman can lay claim to moral superiority by certain austere habits of behavior, plain dress, and frugal living.

It's called Phariseeism because the condition is as old as the Pharisees, written about so angrily in the New Testament. In fact, it probably goes even farther back to the Parsees of ancient India. Pharisees were a religious caste in the Jewish (and Indian) society who lived plainly and had modest incomes, which they believed made them superior to more high-living, highly paid castes in Israel (or India). The Pharisees were particularly called to account by Jesus Christ for their extreme sanctimony, and the certainty that they were better than others.

Pharisaical (*Phariseeism* is another way of spelling *Pharisaism*) classes have existed in almost all societies that we know of, probably because Phariseeism is such a powerful, psychologically satisfying force for many people. Here in America, we have no such official class—but we do have university professors, foundation officials, professional graduate students, university town hangers-on, consumer advocates, mainstream Christian officials, Reform Jewish rabbis, and editorial writers for major newspapers and magazines.

These people are almost always more poorly paid than plastic surgeons or the beautiful people on Wall Street or in law firms, so they can't live in 5,000-square-foot homes or fly first class. They must pass by expensive restaurants and shops and feel the pain of their inability to eat the most expensive foods (except for the rare "nice bottle of Chardonnay" or "good slice of Stilton," which are inexpensive but still show an ability to have good taste, as opposed to the lavish pretentiousness of the rich, who simply throw money at Dom Perignon or Far Niente in their loutish, spendthrift way). But—and this is a big but—such sanctimonious folks can feel that by a glorious kind of moral jiujitsu, their very modesty of means shows that they're morally superior.

What Would Jesus Drive?

The modern-day Pharisee forestalls feelings of envy of the woman in her new 7 Series BMW as he slides by in his rusty, sputtering, 15-year-old Volvo, by telling himself that he's not polluting the earth with eight cylinders of internal combustion. Rather, by only having four cylinders, he's saving the earth. He might feel a bit of envy of the family in the huge new home with its glittering swimming pool while he heads for his hidey-hole of 500 square feet, but he knows in his heart that he's a better person for not using up precious nonrenewable resources by having a pool to heat and a lot of space inside to air-condition. (In fact, the truly Pharisaical person would never dream of even having air-conditioning.)

We all know this type. They explain earnestly that Christ wouldn't condone driving an SUV, thus converting incredibly complex issues of moral worth to a question of miles per gallon. (It's easy to see why Christ so detested the Pharisees.) They sit next to us at stop lights in old Peugeots and beat-up Beetles with bumper stickers that say, "War Is Not the Answer," or "No Drilling in the Arctic National Wildlife Refuge." They march in anti-war parades with signs saying that war is not healthy for children and other living things. (This slogan is one of our favorites. It completely ignores the fact that the man against whom the most recent war was waged, Saddam Hussein, virtually created the practice of torturing and murdering children as they played with their toys. Presumably, that was healthier for children than the U.S. rescuing them from Saddam's brutality.)

Phariseeism is an incredibly potent psychological tool because it converts the material superiority of those better off than the Pharisee into a moral weakness—in other words, it transforms the inability of the Pharisee to get rich into a moral virtue. In its power to turn weakness into strength and strength into weakness, it's an almost perfect psychological defense mechanism. It's easy to see why Phariseeism is so appealing, especially to individuals in havens of fear and insecurity such as university towns. (However, we love universities themselves.)

On a small scale, the Pharisee class salves its wounds by assuming a moral superiority, which doesn't do much damage. It keeps an active used-Volvo market, guarantees patronage at

161

coffee shops near college campuses, and assures demand for Birkenstocks and mountain bikes. However, on a larger scale, it's a toxic brew. The Pharisee class detests much of modern America, supposedly for its wastefulness, pretentiousness, and lavishness. And certainly, there is much to dislike about superfluous displays—Phariseeism aside, there *is* such a thing as sickening excess. (Please see *Town & Country* or *Vanity Fair* magazines.) But when this anger is used as a fig leaf to cover up the jealousy of the "merely" middle class for the upper-middle class or the rich, it's pure hypocrisy and noxiously divisive.

On a large scale, when an entire society is tarred with the brush of immorality for its supposed wastefulness (as in, "the U.S. is an evil giant because it only has 5 percent of the world's people but uses up 25 percent of the world's petroleum"), this is lethal sour grapes. This attitude—that it is moral to criticize and belittle those who have more than we do—is dangerous. Not to mention the fact that envy is a sin, no matter how it gets tarted up as hyper-morality.

(As an aside, it's fascinating how often coveting is mentioned in the Ten Commandments, yet how rarely they mention anything about having swimming pools or eight-cylinder cars. There's not one Commandment in either Testament against high productivity. And Calvinists and other Protestant sects consider this a sign of divine selection. It's also fascinating—and frightening—to note that in the past century, the worst mass murderers in history were extreme ascetics: Hitler was a strict vegetarian who abstained from alcohol and derided those who ate meat; Stalin lived in almost monastic simplicity as he ordered the killings of tens of millions. On the other hand, the two great heroes of the last century, FDR and Churchill, loved champagne and martinis, and FDR even was said to eat off gold plates. People who live well tend to be less angry—or perhaps we should say that differently: angry people tend to be into austere living, while happy people tend to like to live well—and not to want to murder others.)

Again, looking at the small scale, Phariseeism belittles the hard work and creativity that, yes, can make people rich, but also provide progress and prosperity to the entire society. On the large scale again, yes, Americans do have more than other nations, but we got that way through industry, hard work, social discipline, and the adoption of free markets. There are plenty of other countries that are well endowed with rich soil and natural resources yet have done little with them. It's wrong to say that America is wasteful and therefore evil because it uses so much without pointing out that it also produces so much—including a way of life that makes even many of our poor rich by international standards.

This kind of Pharisaical hatred of the U.S. because of our wealth creates a destructive climate of self-loathing and self-doubt, which robs us of the moral confidence we need for the ongoing war against a super-Pharisaical terrorist class in the Islamic nations. (We'll get to this in detail soon. For the moment, let's just say that this belief that people are morally better if they have less, while others are bad if they're prosperous and live well, is a voracious worm eating away at the American apple of strength and vitality.)

Wealthy Pharisees?

To be sure, modern Phariseeism also has its humorous side. As this book is being written, the new fashion in Hollywood is for the very rich to drive cars that either run on electricity from being plugged into the wall, or so-called hybrids that use a combination of gasoline and battery power. Such "conscientiousness" shows the morality of the multimillionaire owners of these vehicles.

Yet do they ever consider that the electricity they get out of that wall socket is generated by immense coal-fired plants out in the desert? Do they ever think that it's funny to drive their Priuses to the Van Nuys airport to get on their private jets, with their mammoth consumption of fuel per passenger (but, hey, don't knock it till you've tried it), or that they might be devouring a lot of resources to heat that ski chalet in Aspen they're heading to or to power those yachts lazing at anchor off St. Bart's?

Well, who knows what they're thinking. But they want the best of both worlds: outlandish wealth and the spending of it, along with the ability to proclaim that they're saving the earth. Hollywood Pharisees are as world-class in the hypocrisy department as humans can get. But ultra-rich Pharisees are nothing new. (One of your authors used to spend time with a Rockefeller, a delightful young woman who endlessly regaled friends with stories of how her relatives in their country homes on thousands of well-tended acres would obsess about having toilets that didn't use too much water.) The tales of the rich are filled with efforts to combine wealth and claims to morality with the grand display of simplicity. One need only see the "simple" Indian jewelry of silver and topaz on the wrists of women getting into Lear 60s to make the point. To see these woman at rallies to save America from the rapacious capitalists of the Bush regime is both hilarious and a powerful emetic.

★ ★ ★

The problems we've discussed in this chapter and the last— envy and its Pendleton-shirt brother, Phariseeism—wouldn't be insurmountable problems by any means in peacetime. After all, they're constants of human nature: They've always been with us, and they always will be with us.

But, of course, we're not at peace. Before we get to that dismal problem, let's consider another danger to the national prognosis for survival: the infantile inability to make moral distinctions.

★★★ ★★★

Chapter

The Moral Blindness of the Left

As this book was being written (in the winter and spring of 2004), a documentary called *Strange Fruit* was making the art-house rounds. The movie tells the story of how the famed Billie Holiday song against lynching came to be written. According to the film, a New York City teacher named Abel Meeropol, a member of the Communist Party of the United States of America, or CPUSA, was (very rightly) upset and offended by lynchings he'd read about or seen in newsreels in the southern states of the U.S. in the mid- and late-1930s. He came home and composed "Strange Fruit," a song that, by various ways and means, made its way through coffeehouses and union halls. It subsequently came to the attention of the great Lady Day, who insisted on recording it against the advice of her managers and record label. Nevertheless, the song, justifiably, became a classic.

Abel Meeropol was a friend and comrade, so to speak, of Julius and Ethel Rosenberg, the couple who, after a lengthy trial, was convicted of spying for the Soviet Union. Specifically, they were found to have worked with a ring of other Communist spies, some in the Manhattan Project, to get vital details of how to make an atomic bomb to Joseph Stalin. This very act dramatically cut the time needed for the Soviets to make a working atomic bomb and to menace the United States and the free world for the next 40 years. (The Rosenbergs were executed for espionage in 1953, at which point Mr. Meeropol and his family adopted Julius and Ethel's children, one of whom helps narrate *Strange Fruit.*)

This film, as noted, is, at the moment, the toast of certain art houses, and the song was a much-needed musical condemnation of a morally repulsive and inexcusable fact of American life for far too long. But what's missing from the documentary, and the acclaim for its makers and the daring Mr. Meeropol, is something startling and deeply upsetting.

How ironic it is that today's moviemakers and cinephiles are paying homage to a man who fought for civil rights for blacks—at the same time that he was an active, committed member of an organization that was a cat's-paw of one of the two worst mass murderers and criminals against human rights in the history of the western world, only matched by Adolf Hitler. How amazing that today liberals are paying acclaim to a man who lived in a society where he was free to complain (and rightly so) about lynchings that claimed several lives a year; meanwhile, he was an active member of a group that sought to destroy that free society and replace it with a totalitarian dictatorship modeled on Stalin's Russia—where tens of millions of innocent men, women, and children were murdered by the twin of the political movement he was in.

That is, Meeropol was part of an anti-human conspiracy so much more vicious and lethal than anything in the U.S. South, that for him to profess to be a friend of human rights is puzzling, if not outright sickening. And the people who praise him and the film about his work generally fail to ever mention this comparison.

Likewise, it certainly was kind of the Meeropol family to adopt the Rosenbergs' two sons, who were absolutely and unequivocally innocent of any crime of any kind. And Meeropol was apparently a devoted and kind father to them, which is to his credit as well. But there's no mention whatsoever of the moral issue of giving key secrets of the atom bomb to one of the two most satanic enemies of human decency in the history of the Western world. Indeed, in the press releases for the documentary, the Rosenbergs are referred to as "atom spies" in quotation marks, perhaps intended to show that the whole case against them was trumped-up, and they were just social and agrarian reformers.

Now, *Strange Fruit* is just one little documentary—it probably won't change the world. But it's richly and sadly symptomatic of a tendency within the liberal establishment and especially its "artistic" wing (two can play the quotation-marks game). That tendency is to forgive and minimize or even ignore the most horrific misconduct imaginable by left-wing regimes while focusing a microscope on the evils of non-left-wing regimes . . . especially on the "evils" of the United States.

For example, it's certainly well known that Stalin's Russia was one of the cruelest regimes in human history—in the scope of its crimes, it easily matches Hitler's unspeakable acts against humanity. Yet while Hollywood has (very rightly) cranked out dozens of films about Nazism (including some startlingly fine ones like *Shoah* and *Schindler's List*), there has been nothing out of Hollywood at all that documents in any detail or with any dramatic vivacity the unspeakable horrors of life under Lenin and Stalin. Why is that? Why is there no *Shoah* about the Gulag? Why is there no *Schindler's List* about the enforced starvation of the brave Ukrainian people, who were so deprived of their own food, grown in their own fields, that they resorted to cannibalism? Why has there been no heartrending multi-part miniseries about the horrors inflicted on Russia by Stalin and Lenin as there have been about the horrors of the Nazis?

There are routinely movies about the oppression and exploitation of women in America; overweight, idiotic, racist sheriffs are standard-issue staples of movies; and businessmen who poison the air and water are as basic to American moviemaking as raw film stock itself. But of the real evils in the world, the ones that truly wrought havoc on human decency, Nazism is a standard—and it should be—but precious little from Communist regimes makes it onto the big (or small) screen.

If Americans got all their information about the world and the 20th century from the mass culture, they'd assume that there were a number of evils in the world in the past hundred years—big business, medium-sized business, small business, American racism, gender oppression—but they'd know nothing about the Communist evil that has claimed the lives of more than 100 million innocent men, women, and children in Russia, China, Eastern Europe, Southeast Asia, Cuba, and elsewhere.

There was a gripping, brilliant Hollywood movie about the horrors and atrocities of the Khmer Rouge Communist regime in Cambodia, a work of art called *The Killing Fields*. But there's never been anything comparable about life in Stalin's Russia, Castro's Cuba, or Mao's China. In the epic classic *The Last Emperor*, the Chinese Communists, who in real life murdered tens of millions, were portrayed as patient teachers. Why? Or, to put it far more starkly, why have there been dozens, perhaps hundreds, of movies and TV shows about the evils of Southern racism in America and not one major American studio production (that we could find, anyway) about what life, torture, and death were like in the days of the terror in Russia or in any parts of the Soviet empire in Eastern Europe?

Even today, when we're at war with Islamic terrorism, there's almost nothing shown about how horrifying life in repressive Islamic regimes is either in the film or television mediums. There are movies about gangsters, drug dealers, and the Ku Klux Klan, and there should be—but where are the pictures depicting the staggering repression of women in fundamentalist Islamic societies? Where is even one Hollywood movie about the vicious cruelty Arab terrorists have visited on Israel?

To anyone who has worked in Hollywood for many years, as one of your authors has, or for even a short time, as the other has, it's obvious that Hollywood is very largely populated and run by Jewish producers, writers, studio executives, and directors. And more power to them. They have created by far the best mass culture apparatus on earth. But when it comes to showing the horrors that Arab murderers have perpetrated on Israel, there is not one movie in theaters or on TV (at least that we could find). Why?

The point here isn't that Hollywood is predominantly left wing—that's so well documented now that it's a cliché. (Anyone doubting it should reference the articles on the "Hate Bush" rally of the beautiful people in Hollywood and Beverly Hills in late 2003.) The point is that Americans need to have some idea of where evil in this world comes from if we're to address it. If our mass culture consistently refuses to show where the primary iniquity of our time comes from, we'll be unable to fight it. Instead, we'll devote our energies to battling trivial and inconsequential problems compared with the life-threatening enemies we actually have.

This is all sadly typical of what much of the Left does in this country. It confuses what is important with what is not. Now, again, to be sure, poverty *is* a real problem—and for the genuinely poor, it's a tragedy. Similarly, there are real issues of domestic violence and environmental issues. (One of your authors spends time

171

in northern Idaho, a magnificent area under constant environmental threat from mining operations.) Perhaps there's even an issue of how many miles per gallon a car should get on the highway.

But compared with the threats from well-organized and rage-filled men in Islamic countries, these are modest problems indeed. To the extent that they divert Americans and subvert our sense of self-confidence, they sap our will to fight. And that's the real problem.

★★★ ★★★

Chapter

The Crux of the Matter

A t this point, we'd like to stop and make a few things perfectly clear. First of all, we don't think that all Democrats are miscreants, traitors, or fools. That would be a wild
misreading of what we have to say. We actually feel that there
are many Democrats and liberals who are extremely fine people. They're good citizens. They take care of their families. They
don't commit crimes or betray their trust in any area of their
lives. In fact, most of the people we know and work with day
by day are Democrats, and they're excellent human beings.
This isn't a book excoriating liberals or Democrats per se by any
possible interpretation.

Second, this isn't a book cataloguing failed liberal social or
foreign policy or defense stands. We assume that liberals make
serious mistakes in those areas, but then those areas are so difficult that we assume that everyone of every political stripe
makes similar errors.

Third, this book isn't meant to imply that the leading
spokespersons of the Democrat/liberal wing of political dis-
course are horrible, disloyal people. We've read books that make

such a case, and their authors are fine people, but that's not our point of view. We have the advantage of knowing some of the leading spokespersons for the Left in this country, and some of them are incredibly decent human beings whom we're proud to call our friends.

For example, one of your authors has occasionally criss-crossed the country to debate with Al Franken. Now, there's much that we disagree on concerning his diagnosis and pre-scription for America, but much of what Al says is sensible as well. And as to his patriotism and devotion to his country, of that there can be little doubt except in the minds of those who don't know him. Al has entertained the troops in some of the most hazardous combat areas of Iraq, and no one can call him anything but a patriot. We have said it before and we will say it again. Likewise, one of your authors worked with Norman Lear, one of the arch liberals in this country, for several years. Nor-man probably stands for almost every size and shape of cause we disagree with in this country. But he flew more than 30 combat bombing missions over Nazi-occupied Europe in World War II, which is a lot more than either of us has ever done for this country. Of his patriotism and full-hearted love of the nation, there can be little doubt.

Fourth, we don't see all the liberals in government as evil peo-ple bent on national destruction. Bill Clinton was in many ways a disturbingly dishonest man. But he made great progress in right-ing this country's fiscal boat, and on a personal level, he was often a kind and generous man. To dismiss him as an enemy of soci-ety is just too easy and not true. His anger and frustration at being caught in a lie is all too human and commonplace a situation, as those of us who have watched Martha Stewart on TV recently can testify. In addition, there are many thoughtful and fine Democrats in Congress even now. The name Bob Kerrey of Nebraska comes to mind: War hero, fiscal conservative, and careful analyst of budgetary matters, he represents a certain kind of man who transcends political labels and rises to genuine national service distinction, although he did not distinguish himself by cursing at Condoleezza Rice on national TV.

Further, we don't see all liberal journalists as cranks and saboteurs. For every Paul Krugman foaming at the mouth to attack Bush and the GOP on any issue at every opportunity, there's an E. J. Dionne, Jr., who sees the world as clearly as he can and genuinely seeks to use his gallon of ink to make a difference for the better.

Both of your authors have close relatives who are liberals, close friends who are liberals, and colleagues who are liberals who have been extremely good to us throughout our lives. One of us worked as a columnist under the great liberal editor and original thinker in journalism, Jim Bellows of *New York* magazine, the *New York Herald Tribune,* and the late, great *Los Angeles Herald-Examiner*. He was also a hero in World War II. To say that a man like that is in any sense less than a devoted, brave, and intelligent patriot is simple nonsense.

The people we're worried about are the ones who never build up but only pull down. We're concerned about the people whose hatred of the United States and her free-market system and need for a powerful defense is unrelenting. We're talking about the people who can't see an American flag without feeling shame and rage, who see so much gender oppression here that they can't draw a meaningful line between the Islamic societies that make women into slaves and the American society that makes women into icons and goddesses.

We're troubled about the people who see nothing redemptive or magical about the American experience, who see America as a late link in the unending chain of capitalist (or male) oppression and seek, like al-Qaeda, to tear down and never to enhance or improve.

175

And here we come to the crux of the matter.

America's Real Problem

Neither of your authors would for a moment doubt that there's plenty that needs to be done to make this a better nation. For the most overwhelming example, take abortion. No nation that has a Supreme Court that sanctions the mass murder of innocent children by the millions mainly because they're embarrassing or inconvenient can hope to be anything resembling a highly moral society. For as long as the U.S. is soaked in the blood of unborn babies, it's simply impossible to call it anything close to perfection.

In addition, while poverty isn't as bad as some complainers make it out to be, in a nation as wealthy as this one is—one that boasts five or ten million millionaire families (by different methods of calculation) and hundreds of billionaires (many of whom pay little tax)—there's no excuse for denying health-care coverage to the tens of millions of poor families who desperately need it. And as we've said before, there are also environmental problems, although, to be sure, they're in the context of a rapidly improving picture. (Nevertheless, this country's natural beauty is such a vital part of our national heritage that the strictest scrutiny is merited on whether harm to the environment is really needed.)

But the real problem in this country is exposed when anger over these matters gets so intense and bitter that it interferes with the critical item on our national and international agenda: defending our nation from the Islamic terrorists who want to end our free society, our religious, ethnic, and gender progress. Those people, who see America as the real source of all evil, are the genuine dangers to our society—and human decency in the world—for the foreseeable future.

To put it in another way, every one of the complaints about America that we've laid out in this book (and there are many others we could have included) is a standard part of post-1960s America; none of them would be a major problem or concern if we were at peace. In other words, we could handle nutty people carrying around placards warning about the "horrors" of globalization and explaining that America is the Great Satan; and we could deal with Looney Tunes-type individuals blowing their tops about the supposed wickedness of racism and how any self-respecting person should hate America because of its bigotry, *if* we weren't at war with those who really mean to put an end to this country and our way of life.

September 11, 2001, put us in a new situation. Ever since, we've been at war with what is the most resourceful and conscienceless enemy we've faced in the postwar world; in many ways, we're facing the most dangerously invasive enemy we have *ever* faced.

Historians generally agree that Hitler and Hirohito had no plans to occupy the United States of America and kill civilians on a mass scale. No one has ever been able to come up with a plan by the Nazis to create a national Socialist, Jew-free America. Even in the details of Hitler's most intimate conversation, no mention of an attack on America has ever been found.

The Soviets had an active espionage operation and a totally subservient Communist Party that would have loved to take over America. But as far as anyone knows, Stalin had no imminent plans to attack New York. (Although very recent research shows that in his later, most demented years, Stalin might well have been entertaining nuclear war as a possibility, but this is just speculation so far.)

Certainly, when we were fighting in Vietnam, we faced a resourceful and cruel foe. But no one has ever intimated that the North Vietnamese planned to take a fleet of rafts across the Pacific, through the Panama Canal, and up the East Coast to attack the Pentagon. Once we left Vietnam, there was no danger of the combat spreading to the United States.

But we're now engaged in a war in which the first battle—a losing one for the United States—was fought in New York City; in Arlington, Virginia; and over the skies of rural Pennsylvania. This is a whole different ball game.

Tearing Ourselves Apart

Today, the people we're fighting are numerous, incredibly desperate, and unafraid of death . . . and they apparently believe that they've only just begun to fight. However many of them there are in al-Qaeda, public-opinion data tell us that there are hundreds of millions more in the Islamic countries that support their war on us. The numbers of the terrorists and their supporters are literally limitless. Their access to money, often derived from our purchases of gasoline and home heating oil, is inexhaustible. Their determination to acquire nuclear weapons is demonstrable and eerily plausible of fulfillment. Even as this is being written, details of a Pakistani nuclear scientist who eagerly sold the know-how of making nuclear weapons to terrorists are in the news. How long until the terrorists and their allies have a nuclear bomb and can carry it to the Port Authority in New York City and set it off? A long time, we hope, but you never know. . . .

To be sure, the U.S. and our coalition won a swift victory in Iraq—but the terrorism there continues at a frightening pace. It was a daring gamble for Mr. Bush to fight over there, but he had great motives to do so. Despite what the naysayers and Monday-morning quarterbacks are saying now, the entire world believed that Saddam Hussein had dangerous chemical and biological weapons before we invaded, and the case that he definitely didn't hasn't thoroughly been made. If Saddam had indeed possessed these weapons, we would have been staring at catastrophe if he'd given them to al-Qaeda to use against the West. Moreover, Saddam had been a constant threat to the oil supplies to which the U.S. has become addicted. He'd already invaded two of our major oil suppliers, Iran and Kuwait—how long until he tried to attack Saudi Arabia and cut off the West's major supplier of oil?

Most daring of all, the President saw that the terrorism and extremism that came out of the Middle East and the Muslim world might have their roots in the dictatorial nature of those nations' regimes. In a bold stroke that Woodrow Wilson would have understood, Bush sought to take one of the worst of the Arab world's dictatorships and remake it into a democracy. In this way, he might pave the way for the democratization of the entire Islamic world, and an end to the political frustration that breeds terrorism—and he might have begun the process of draining the swamps that breed homicide bombers.

Again, to be sure, this was a bold series of moves, and it may well work in the long run. But in the short run, we're still seeing horrifyingly numerous terrorist acts. And the ability of terrorists to strike on a worldwide basis seems to be frighteningly real, if the endless stream of attacks in Iraq and the former Soviet Union are any indication.

Polling of the Muslim world shows terrifying hostility toward the United States, even in nations like Indonesia that used to be friendly to us. Interestingly enough, the roots of anti-Americanism there are much like those same roots here: intense envy, including jealousy of our prosperity and technological progress, and jealousy and fear of our political openness. (These are the very same factors that lead to intense Arab hatred of Israel.)

Added to those motives for hating America is another powerful moving force: fear of the sexuality of women. One of the key elements in many of the nations where anti-Western feeling runs strong is the repression of women's sexual power. When the male leaders of the Muslim states behold America and its freedom for women, they're deeply concerned about what this would do to their dominance if it spread to their lands. If they can repress that force that scares them so much, they'll be relieved. If women's rights, especially their ability to express themselves sexually, came to their nations, they'd have to face a seismic change in their lives.

Now, to be sure, the United States and the West would generally seem to have an immense edge in the struggle against the terrorists and their backers: We're by far the dominant economic and military power on the planet (although hobbled by dependence on foreign energy sources); we're by far the richest large nation on earth; and we're by far the most technologically advanced nation on earth. In any combat in which the United States is fully committed, there can be little doubt of the outcome. Yes, there are about four times as many Muslims as there are citizens of the United States, but by no means are all of these Muslims hostile (or at least actively hostile) to our country—in fact, many of them are friendly to us. But even those many millions of Muslims who *are* energetically hostile to the United States aren't very organized, and only a small percentage of them are organized in any militarily or terroristically dangerous fashion. Yet, as we have seen, even 19 of them with sufficient imagination and willpower can cause tremendous damage.

However, the damage they can do to us, even if armed with terrible weapons, isn't anywhere near as great as what we facilitate ourselves with sufficient self-loathing and homegrown anti-Americanism. Long ago, even before he became President, Abraham Lincoln explained this eloquently. In 1838, the very young man noted that the U.S. was a vast continental nation between two broad oceans, with immense natural resources. He said, "If destruction be our lot, we must ourselves be its author and finisher. As a nation of freemen we must live through all time or die by suicide." But 25 years later, the nation did come very close to breaking apart permanently as internal hostility and anger led to the worst crisis in American history, the Civil War. This is the precedent that so frightens us.

If this country becomes so divided and rent by internal criticism, rage, and self-loathing, to the point that we can no longer resist the physical attacks and moral challenges leveled against us by Islamic terrorists, we could find ourselves in the kind of crisis we mentioned at the beginning of this book: facing a mortal external enemy who will stop at nothing to destroy as much of this country as he can, while we're torn by internal criticism to the point that we can't and don't resist that destruction.

The United States lost roughly 1 out of every 20 males to wounds and disease during the Civil War (amazingly, the Southern states lost close to 1 in 12 men of any age and roughly 1 in 5 of prime military age). *Yet this disaster didn't have to happen.* There were other nations in which slavery was done away with by peaceful means—but the anger on both sides of this country was so severe and out of control that it barred a peaceful solution to the crisis.

When we look out at America today, especially in some of the most frothing quarters of the Left, we see the same sort of anger. An uncompromising, rage-filled, bloodshot-eyed fury fills the air in some quarters when the name of Bush is even brought up. This is dangerous and even disastrous. Of course, criticism and constructive comment is the American way—but the kind of mad hostility we've detailed in the previous chapters is the prelude to national self-destruction.

We face people with a seemingly bottomless wish to harm and kill America and Americans. They believe that it's their religious duty to do so. If we hate ourselves and see ourselves as morally evil—just as they see us—we're in dire straits. We'll end up facing an enemy on the outside *and* on the inside, with results that are hard to predict.

This is especially true if there are more attacks like 9/11; or, again, if the anger of the most bitter critics is turned toward the U.S. instead of the people attacking her. It's trite but urgently true (as Martin Luther King, Jr., said) that a house divided against itself cannot stand (as Abraham Lincoln said). This is especially right on if some madmen with hijacked jets and dangerous weapons are hammering against that house with sledgehammers.

So how do we help the house stand up?

★★★ ★★★

Chapter

Can America Survive?

America is under attack. We're under violent, armed attack from Islamic terrorists; and we're under attack from the seeds of self-doubt, self-loathing, and confusion sown by homegrown troublemakers in universities, in Hollywood, in foundations, in the media, and worst of all, in some of the almost-mainstream groups that have attached themselves to one of our political parties.

Or, to put it another way, we're under attack by men and women who hate America. Consequently, those of us who love this country must love it more than the haters hate it in order for our nation and our free society to be saved.

Now, the Islamic terrorists who hate America despise her so much that nothing we can imagine could make them stop. Osama bin Laden and his ilk want a world of terror, totalitarian repression of anything but their own brand of Islam, and the most violent subjugation of women. They correctly gauge that the American way of life will be ruinous to their way of life and death—that is, if our equality of opportunity, freedom of religion, and prosperity through free markets reach their fiefs, they will be doomed. There is no place for dictators; bigots; and haters of women, Jews, Christians, and peace-loving Muslims in tomorrow's world if it is made on the American model.

This means that the war to defend America against terrorism must go on for a long time. It's very clear that this war must be fought primarily by America, with the help of freedom-loving nations. The UK and other nations that love freedom will cooperate in a major way—but the main burden will be on America.

That's why keeping American resolve strong is indispensable to winning the war on terrorism. And, again, this is what this book is about. We wanted to explain to our fellow Americans why we should be proud of our country, and why we feel that our way of life is worth fighting for ceaselessly (that is, until the world is a safer place). There is some question as to whether it will ever be as safe a place as it was in 1994, before the evil genies of terrorism were loosed from their hellholes in the Middle East and West Asia. But the world *is* safer now that the terror networks themselves are under attack, rather than America playing victim as these malcontents roam freely around the world.

How do we do we keep our resolve strong?

The Value of Education

The primary way to keep our country strong and maintain our belief in ourselves is through education.

There was a time in this country when American children were routinely taught that the USA was the greatest nation in history, the "shining city on the hill" (to use Ronald Reagan's phrase) that would light the way for the entire world. Both of your authors were fortunate enough to be raised in that world.

If you bear in mind the circumstances in which we grew up, you'll be able to see how things have changed.

When your authors were in elementary school in the 1950s and early 1960s, there was simply no doubt that America was the salvation of mankind. When we were kids (Ben Stein in suburban Maryland outside Washington, D.C., and Phil DeMuth in suburban Illinois outside Chicago), our country had recently been victorious in World War II. America had mobilized to fight against genocidal regimes in Europe and East Asia, and our fathers had gone off to war to protect our country and liberate the subjugated parts of the earth. We also had friends whose fathers never returned from Europe or Asia.

The entire civilized world had seen what happened when freedom was extinguished and human rights were trampled. The piles of corpses at Belsen, the Bataan Death March, the use of captured Chinese for bayonet practice by the Japanese, the demolition of Warsaw, the destruction of the majority of European Jewry, the mass murders of the Eastern European peoples—all of this was fresh in our minds and hearts.

We were also taught, in unequivocal terms, what Communism meant. We knew about the enforced starvation in the Ukraine and other portions of the USSR. We knew about the Leninist terrors and the knock on the door in the middle of the night in Stalin's and Beria's Russia. We knew what Red Bolshevism meant in terms of the slaughter of tens of millions of innocent people.

We knew that the U.S. had been allied with Stalin against an even more imminent threat, Hitlerism, but we knew what Communism was. We were taught that Stalin had turned one of the most culturally vibrant and intellectually thriving areas of the globe, Eastern Europe, into a vast penitentiary. We were told about families who had crossed rivers under gunfire to escape Communism. We knew about the uprisings in Lodz and

Budapest against Communism, and how the Russians had brutally suppressed them.

We also knew that Mao Tse-tung's Communists had made much of China into a slaughterhouse after his victory against the corrupt Nationalists of Chiang Kai-shek. Millions who simply weren't workers or peasants met a grisly death under Mao's dictatorship.

So when we looked around us, we saw a free world led by the United States. It looked awfully good compared with what we saw on the rest of the planet. The totalitarian areas were subject to slavery, murder, a lack of legal rights, poverty, and fear; while we had abundant food, suburban homes, freedom of expression and religion, and rock 'n' roll.

One of your authors is Jewish, and he had a very clear idea of what his fate would have been had he been unfortunate enough to have been born in Europe in November of 1944 instead of at Garfield Hospital in Washington, D.C. He also had a very good idea of what had happened to his distant relatives who didn't emigrate from Russia to the United States in the late 19th century. It was impressed upon him in every Sunday School class at the Montgomery County Jewish Community Center that the fate of Jews in Eastern Europe was torment and death. The fate of Jews in Silver Spring, Maryland, on the other hand, was overwhelming comfort, although with occasional jeers and anti-Semitism. Overall, it was a comfortable, safe way of life.

This, basically, was what was taught to us: that the U.S. was a safe place in a very dangerous world. That in itself is more than enough reason to be permanently grateful to America and to love her dearly.

We were also taught, and could see around us, that America wasn't perfect. Mistreatment of blacks was a serious blight on the American ideal. It was a hellish way of life for many people of color. But we were instructed to believe that Americans had the capacity to educate ourselves about a moral problem and then solve it.

Thus, we saw (especially the one of your authors who grew up in Maryland and spent much time in Virginia) that segregation was wrong and oppressive, but that it could also be overcome and eventually consigned to the dustbin of history. We saw terrible wrongs perpetrated against blacks here in our beautiful country, but we also witnessed a heroic band of Americans who would fight those evils and make them a thing of the past. Those wrongs would then be corrected by good people across the political spectrum, from the far Left to the solid pro-civil-rights Republican party of Dwight Eisenhower, Richard Nixon, Nelson Rockefeller, and Ronald Reagan.

We'd been taught history, so we knew that slavery was a moral crime that had been committed against blacks and against the American ideal, and it was a thing of hideous ugliness. But we also knew well that the freedom of blacks had been bought with the blood of hundreds of thousands of white men. This, we knew, was a situation such as had never happened in history before: that men of one race would leave their homes to fight and die to liberate men of another race from bondage by men of their own race. The Southern earth was drenched with the blood of blacks drawn by the lash, to coin a phrase by Lincoln— but it was also honored by the blood of brave men who had fought to find freedom for total strangers.

When we grew up, our parents used to utter a phrase describing how wonderful life was here: It simply was, "Only in America." Only in America could people like the Steins, who came from the most modest ancestry in Russia and the Baltic states, have enjoyed education, prosperity, a place at the table of top advisers to Presidents, spots at prestigious colleges, and a full dinner plate every night. Only in America could a Jew feel safe that

187

he'd never be the object of a pogrom. Only in America could the DeMuths, of modest Moravian ancestry, find prosperity, shelter, social position, and places at the finest private schools and in the councils of state that determined how America would be run.

Earlier we mentioned a conversation that one of your authors, Ben Stein, had with his father around 1970. To paraphrase, Herbert Stein had told his son, "Benjy, never in history has any group in America—blacks, Italians, Asians, Irish, English, or Jews—lived as well as they live in America." But then he added something else a moment later, "Of all the accomplishments that any Stein has ever had, none compares with your grandparents and great-grandparents coming to America." His wife, Mildred Stein, added, "Once you're in America, it's all good fortune after that."

It is to this level of pride in the nation that we must strive to return. It is with this level of confidence that "we're right, and our enemies are wrong" that we must fight the war on terror. But how do we get there?

Again, education. At some point, American schools stopped teaching patriotism and began telling kids that it's a racist, anti-woman, imperialist state. Gone were the centuries of teaching how uniquely blessed we are to be Americans, replaced by volumes about what was wrong with this country.

Excellent Sources of Patriotism

It's now our job to replenish the stocks of patriotism and belief in America; then we must pass this belief on to our children and to others who need guidance. The drill is similar to what we're told to do if an airplane we're on loses pressurization: Attach the air mask to *our* faces first, and then attach the masks to our children.

To do this, above all, it's necessary to read. It isn't enough to have been educated properly 40 years ago or more. We have to keep educating ourselves about the glory of America's history and about the facts of our freedom, prosperity, and moral leadership right now.

Below, we recommend a few sources that have gripped our attention and morally rearmed us. (There will be a list of these at the end of this book, but we'd like to note a few here, broken down by subject.)

The Civil War

An epic poem by Stephen Vincent Benet about the origins and tragedy of the Civil War, called *John Brown's Body,* was once standard issue for American readers, but it has now sadly drifted out of fashion. This is too bad, for it's a powerful and brilliantly moving work. (We suspect that *Gone with the Wind* was largely inspired by it, but we don't know that for a fact. In any event, *John Brown's Body* doesn't suffer from the race stereotyping and bias that make *Gone with the Wind* so problematic in modern life.)

Within the last decade, a superb book about the Civil War has come out that traces the American devotion to freedom in extreme detail but is written to be a compelling read: James McPherson's *Battle Cry of Freedom.* It's an inspiring book, especially in its lengthy discussion of the American need to free the enslaved pitted against the horrible history of Negro bondage. And the entire series of Civil War books by Bruce Catton is a quick but detailed and moving excursion into the history of this nation in its greatest crisis.

There are also two fine magazines about the Civil War that do justice to the heroism on both sides, and also note the immense contribution (often overlooked) that black Americans made in securing their own freedom. We suggest *Civil War Times* and *America's Civil War,* as they feature a wealth of glorious and tragic articles telling how America made good on its pledge to promote freedom and equality.

World War II

There are so many wonderful books on the Second World War that there would be no way to list them all here. A recent, highly moving one is *Flags of Our Fathers* by Bradley and Powers. This book, which tells the story of the men who raised the Stars and Stripes over the blood-soaked summit of Mount Suribachi on Iwo Jima in 1945, as well the whole history of the war in the Pacific, is thoroughly inspiring. It explains how much blood had to be poured into the red sand of Iwo Jima to achieve victory against one of the most dangerous forces in human history: Japanese imperialism. It's also a telling tale of how difficult the transitions of the three Marines from that famous picture were when they came back from Iwo Jima, as well as how much sacrifice is required for people to live in peace. One of the authors of this book, James Bradley, also wrote a great book about U.S. flyers in World War II (including George H. W. Bush) called *Flyboys.*

One of the classics about the war from the German side offers a blood-curdling view into just how horrible, yet idiotic, the Third Reich was. *The Rise and Fall of the Third Reich* by William L. Shirer is a must-read to show us yet again just how blessed we are to live where we do and to have defeated the Nazi war machine, which was an extremely formidable organism.

The late Stephen Ambrose published a series of serviceable and impressive (if not original) books about World War II.

Band of Brothers is a particularly good one, and was made into a superb television series of the same name. Unfortunately, it was running when the catastrophe of September 11 happened, so it lost much of its audience.

There is also a spectacularly good magazine about World War II called (appropriately enough) *World War II*. Almost every month it features brilliant stories about American heroism and sacrifice in that global war. (As this book was being written, the magazine featured a heart-rending article called "Bataan Death March Poet," briefly describing the story of a young Marine named Henry Lee from South Pasadena, California. This brave young man kept a journal and wrote poetry about his unbearable suffering at the hands of the Japanese in their captivity after his capture in early 1942. His once widely read poems reflect a level of sensitivity and courage that's almost beyond belief. You might be able to find them on a used-book site under the name *Nothing But Praise*.)

In the early 1950s, NBC put out a series about World War II, especially the naval side of the war, entitled *Victory at Sea*. Shot in glorious black and white, it has some of the most moving scenes and dialogue of how the war unfolded and was won by American determination, heroism, and self-sacrifice. Viewing this series is an ideal way for a family to spend some time together. At the end of the 24 half-hour episodes, you'll have a much better picture of what America went through to get us to the blessed victory over Germany and Japan than you did when you went in (unless you started out as a history buff).

In the same vein is *Battlefield,* a series of videos of the great battles and campaigns of World War II that were fought all around the world. Some of the campaigns have little to do with the U.S., but the ones that do, such as those about Leyte Gulf, are magnificent. Each episode is one hour long and contains a rich trove of data and inspiration.

Communism

Probably the single most important book we've ever read is *The Russian Century,* by a British author and journalist named Brian Moynahan. This astounding book tells the story of what life and death in Russia were like, starting with the first stirrings of the most evil doctrine in history, Communism. To read about the terrors inflicted on the superhumanly brave Russian people by Lenin, Stalin, and some (but not all) of their successors is to be staggered by the ability of man to inflict pain on other men. The richly illustrated version (complete with photos of Ukrainians reduced to cannibalism by Stalin's enforced starvation of their country) is out of print, but a paperback version without many illustrations is readily available. You'll never have a moment's sympathy for Communism or Socialism if you dare to read this book. You'll feel in your gut just how horrible a fate we escaped by fighting and winning the Cold War.

In a similar vein, with an even broader scope, is Stephane Courtois et al.'s master work, *The Black Book of Communism.* This French (yes, French) editor catalogues the casualty rate from Communism in this century, putting it at between 85 and 100 million innocent souls. To read this book is to be aghast that so many Americans still defend Communism as an ideologically noble endeavor.

Gulag, by Anne Applebaum, is also a marvelously (and agonizingly detailed) account of how the vast prison system worked in the Soviet Union—extinguishing hope, life, and decency even as the best and brightest defended Stalin in the U.S. and Great Britain.

Books like these, as well as an entire series by the great historians John Earl Haynes and Harvey Klehr, illustrate how totally hoodwinked the intellectual class in America often was—and how often that class went to bat for Soviet mass murder even when they knew what was happening. These books make clear how vital it is that ordinary Americans make up their own minds to defend the nation and not leave it up to the teachers.

The Civil Rights Movement

Eyes on the Prize is an inspiring documentary, available on DVD and video, showing how battles for the Civil Rights movement were fought in the 1950s and 1960s. It's depressing at first, but it's ultimately uplifting in the way that it shows Americans fighting to liberate other Americans, always with the watchwords of *equality* and *freedom* uppermost in their minds. It's also an inspiration to see how Martin Luther King, Jr., used nonviolence to achieve his goals. As he often said, "Moral ends to reach moral means."

Other Resources

There are a couple current books about America that are extremely worth your time. First is a book of statistics that only the most hard-core readers will get, but it's worth it. It's called the *Statistical Abstract of the United States* and is published every year by the Government Printing Office. To rummage through it and see how much progress has been made in education, family income, housing, and health is to be inspired by what America has accomplished. The numbers tell a deeply impressive tale. Second, a recent book by our friend Dinesh D'Souza, called *What's So Great About America,* lays out in convincing form just how well America is doing by historic and geographic standards. It's a short, pleasant read.

There are also some great newspapers that take a consistently pro-American point of view and instill a sense of the greatness of the nation in readers. The number one most vital daily read is *The Wall Street Journal,* especially the editorial page. There, every Monday through Friday, you can learn the side of the story that the major networks will never tell you, including how dangerous the Left can be, especially when it's working hand in glove with the Islamic terror network; how the Left lies about foreign policy (as when John Kerry makes up conversations with foreign leaders who supposedly tell him they can't wait for him to be President), how the court system is wreaking havoc on our laws and morals, and other vital subjects.

No one in this country who really values his or her birthright as an American should be without the *Journal's* editorial page on a daily basis. (Point of full disclosure: this book's co-author Ben Stein was a columnist and editorial writer for the page long ago and is still among its most devout fans.) In addition, *The Washington Times,* which is available by mail and online, is relentless in prying open scandals among liberals, making for stunning reading. It's unfashionable, but then so is patriotism.

Among magazines, there are several gems. Naturally, we heartily recommend *The American Spectator.* (Again, full disclosure: Ben Stein has been writing for this magazine for more than 30 years.) It's fearless in confronting the hypocrisy and double-dealing of the liberals, and will take on the most wildly sacred cows such as diversity. It played a large part in opening the public's eyes about Clinton (whom we don't really dislike as much as some do, but we're awfully glad that he's no longer in office). Its editors, Bob Tyrrell and Wlady Pleszczynzski, are talented and fearless.

The *National Review* is the gold standard in conservative magazines and is by far the oldest. Unabashedly pro-God and pro-American, it takes on anyone who crosses the line into foolishness, subjugation, and hate as fair game. This magazine isn't afraid in the least to take on George W. Bush on immigration issues, but that's another book. Rich Lowry, the editor, is a genius; and the founding father, Bill Buckley, is an inspiration decade after decade.

The Weekly Standard is a small, brilliantly worked-out magazine edited by many friends of ours. Take it with you everywhere you go (it can easily be read on a medium-length plane ride).

Finally, *The American Enterprise,* published by Christopher DeMuth, the brother of one of your authors, is a rich source of sense and sensibility, and it's especially useful for its excellent statistics on polling data. Subscribe to all of these, discuss them within your family, and give them as gift subscriptions—they'll keep you centered around gratitude and patriotism.

✳ ✳ ✳

These books, videos, and periodicals are just a start, but they're enough to tell us how magnificent America is. They also let us know how vital it is that we absorb the truth about our nation and then pass this on to our children and our friends. There are many people who are so filled with anger (and themselves) that they can't possibly be converted to love their own country. But there are also many on the fence who would like information, to be convinced, and to be shown the truth about their country. So when we have the facts and the concepts in hand, we should share them with the people close to us. Little by little, the message will get passed around, and it will stick where needed. Or so we hope.

Other Steps to Take

Prayer works. If we truly believe, as we should, that this nation enjoys a special providence from God, then we owe it to the Creator to thank Him every day, many times a day, for the greatness of our lives here in America. It's very clear that He's intervened over and over again to bless this nation. All you have to do is look around you—compare your life with those of other people you see on the news, and you'll get a darned good idea of the blessings He has showered upon us.

When we're in crisis (as we are now), we need to pray. All the great leaders of this country have been men of faith. It's deeply inspiring to read about George Washington kneeling in the snow at Valley Forge to pray for the survival of the fledgling nation's tiny army; or to know that Abraham Lincoln spent many of the darkest days of the Civil War on his knees in supplication to the Almighty, often invoking Him in his remarks. To see the newsreels of Winston Churchill and FDR praying together for the success and survival of the English-speaking democracies is an impressive sight. And George W. Bush has confessed that he asks for Divine guidance on a daily basis (there's a fine book on this subject entitled *A Man of Faith* by David Aikman). Those of us who love America can do no less.

Also, take a hand in your children's education. Ask to see the list of books that will be studied in their history, world civilization, civics, and English classes. If they're all anti-American and anti-freedom books that mock and belittle our country, suggest some alternatives. If you feel that you've read or experienced enough to be able to talk to the students at your nearby school, volunteer to be a speaker about some aspect of the United States experience that you know well. This is a particularly apt suggestion for current and former military men and women. The true stories of their experiences in combat to keep

America free are vital and invaluable—these firsthand stories can influence students far more than any textbook.

All of the above applies to the college level as well. There's no reason not to write to your children's instructors and ask them to consider using some of the books you've read that instill pride in our nation. If the professor mocks and then ignores you—a real possibility in today's universities—then offer the books to your child/student yourself with a request that he or she read them. Not all children belittle all that's suggested to them by their parents. Take a chance.

Get subscriptions to *The Wall Street Journal* and to the magazines we mentioned above for your kids if they're away at school, and for your school's libraries. Even the most sullen child who's exposed to patriotic sources on a weekly basis will learn something. Teach your kids about their ancestors and their exploits in the Old Country, or here in this one. Teach them what your parents and grandparents did in World War II, Korea, Vietnam, the Cold War, or in whatever forum they fought for America. And above all, teach pride—don't allow your kids to feel shame (except about abortion).

Support candidates you believe in. If you want men and women elected who believe in what you do, it's your job to get it done. Elections are lost because patriotic Americans assume that someone else will do it. That isn't so—it's not someone else's job; it's yours. So pass out literature, contribute what you can, make phone calls, ring doorbells, sign petitions, and so on. Get into the arena and work for what you believe in. And above all, vote. Brave men died to allow us to govern ourselves, so it's up to us to vindicate their belief and trust in the democratic system of a self-governing republic.

Support our troops: Give to the USO; get letters out to service-people, and send them DVDs, video games, and books. Make certain they know you care about them—and make sure that their families are never lonely or in need. There are groups like the Folded Flag Foundation that take up collections for those families who have lost a dear one in foreign fields. Give to and help them.

Don't let TV commentators get away with lies about our country. If you see someone telling a falsehood about America or about the way you know it to be, call them on it. Make sure they get mail setting them straight. Both of your authors have worked in the media, and we know that people in it are sensitive to complaints. They want to be liked, even by you and me. If we make it clear that we don't like their attitude, we can sometimes get it changed.

Never give up. America is the hope for the entire future of mankind. But there are far too many men and women in far too many positions of power who want to see America stumble and fall from grace. The decent ones, often the "little people" who are far from the corridors of power but who keep the society running at the local police station, firehouse, bank, or hospital are the backbone of the nation. They can and do make it work, and they protect and preserve it.

The future of eight billion souls—the entire human race—rests on the shoulders and in the hearts of those who still believe in this great country. Be one of them for your entire life. Give up, and the battle is lost, along with mankind's future. Keep the faith, and the nation will still be here, a shining city on a hill for your grandchildren and their grandchildren.

★★★ ★★★

APPENDIX

BIBLIOGRAPHY

Aikman, David. *A Man of Faith: The Spiritual Journey of George W. Bush.* Nashville, TN: W Publishing Group, 2004.

Ambrose, Stephen E. *Band of Brothers.* New York: Simon & Schuster, 2001.

The American Enterprise: **www.taemag.com**

The American Spectator: **www.spectator.org**

America's Civil War magazine. New York: Primedia. Subscriptions: (800) 829-3340.

Applebaum, Anne. *Gulag: A History.* New York: Doubleday, 2003.

Bailey, Ronald, ed. *Global Warming and other Eco-Myths.* Roseville, CA: Prima Publishing, 2002.

Barber, Benjamin R. *Jihad vs. McWorld.* New York: Ballantine Books, 1996.

Battlefield. Polygram/Time-Life Video, La Mancha Productions, 1994.

Benet, Stephen Vincent. *John Brown's Body.* Chicago, IL: Ivan R. Dee, 1990.

Billingsly, Kenneth Lloyd. *Hollywood Party: How Communism Seduced the American Film Industry in the 1930s and 1940s.* Roseville, CA: Prima Lifestyles, 1998.

Bloch, Sidney; and Reddaway, Peter. *Psychiatric Terror: How Soviet Psychiatry Is Used to Suppress Dissent.* New York: Basic Books, 1977.

Bradley, James. *Flags of our Fathers.* New York: Delacorte, 2001.

——. *Flyboys.* Boston, MA: Little, Brown, 2003.

Caplow, Theodore; Hicks, Louis; and Wattenberg, Ben J. *The First Measured Century: An Illustrated Guide to Trends in America, 1900–2000.* Washington, D.C.: AEI Press, 2000.

Carson, Rachel. *Silent Spring.* Boston: Houghton-Mifflin, 1962.

Catton, Bruce. *The Civil War*. New York: American Heritage, 1985.

Center for American Women and Politics, Eagleton Institute of Politics–Rutgers: **http://www.cawp.rutgers.edu**

Chairman, Council of Economic Advisors. *Economic Report of the President 2003*. Washington, D.C.: U.S. Government Printing Office, 2003.

Charen, Mona. *Useful Idiots: How Liberals Got It Wrong in the Cold War and Still Blame America First*. Washington, D.C.: Regnery Publishing, 2003.

Christy, J.R., et al. "Error Estimates of Version 5.0 of MSU-AMSU Bulk Atmospheric Temperatures." *Journal of Atmospheric and Oceanic Technology* 20:613–629. 2003

Civil War Times. New York: Primedia. Subscriptions: (800) 829-3340.

Committee on the Science of Climate Change, National Research Council. *Climate Change Science: An Analysis of Some Key Questions*. Washington, D.C.: National Academy Press, 2001.

Coulter, Ann. *Slander*. New York: Crown, 2002.

——. *Treason*. New York: Crown, 2003.

Courtois, Stephane (ed.); Kramer, Mark (trans.); Murphy, Jonathan (trans.); Werth, Nicolas; Panne, Jean-Louis; Paczkowski, Andrzei; Bartosek, Karel; and Margolin, Jean-Louis. *The Black Book of Communism*. Cambridge, MA: Harvard University Press, 1999.

Cox, W. Michael; and Alm, Richard. *Myths of Rich and Poor: Why We're Better Off Than We Think*. New York: Basic Books, 2000.

Deming, David. "Are We Running Out of Oil?" National Center for Policy Analysis, May 2003 • **http://www.flinthills.org/Publications/General%20Policy/Run%20out%20oil.htm**

Department of Labor, Bureau of Labor Statistics. *Consumer Expenditure Survey*. Washington, D.C.: Government Printing Office, 2004.

Doran, P.T.; Priscu, J.C; Lyons, W.B.; Walsh, J.E.; Fountain, A.G.; McKnight, D.M.; Moorhead, D.L.; Virginia, R.A.; Wall, D.H.; Clow, G.D.; Fritsen, C.H.; McKay, C.P.; and Parsons, A.N. "Antarctic Climate Cooling and Terrestrial Ecosystem Response." *Nature* 415:517–520. 2002.

D'Souza, Dinesh. *The End of Racism: Principles for a Multiracial Society*. New York: Free Press, 1996.

——. *What's So Great About America?* Washington, D.C.: Regnery Publishing, 2002.

Ehrlich, Paul. *The Population Bomb*. New York: Ballantine Books, 1968.

Eyes on the Prize. PBS Home Video, 1995.

Federal Reserve Board. *2001 Survey of Consumer Finances*.

Fumento, Michael. *Bioevolution: How Biotechnology is Changing our World*. San Francisco, CA: Encounter Books, 2003.

Furchtgott-Roth, Diana; and Stolba, Christine. *Women's Figures: An Illustrated Guide to the Economic Progress of Women in America*. Washington, D.C.: AEI Press, 1999.

Gore, Al. *Earth in the Balance: Ecology and the Human Spirit*. Boston: Houghton-Mifflin, 1992.

Gwartney, James; and Lawson, Robert. *Economic Freedom of the World: 2003 Annual Report*. Fraser Institute, 2003 • Website: **http://www.freetheworld.com**

Haynes, John Earl; and Klehr, Harvey. *Venona: Decoding Soviet Espionage in America*. New Haven, CT: Yale University Press, 1999.

Heimann, Jim. *All American Ads*. Koln, Germany: Taschen, 2002.

Johnson, Paul. *Intellectuals*. New York: Harper & Row, 1988.

Jost, John T.; Glaser, Jack; Kruglanski, Arie W.; and Sulloway, Frank J. "Political Conservatism as Motivated Social Cognition." *Psychological Bulletin*: 2003 Vol. 129, No. 3, pp. 339–374.

Klehr, Harvey; Haynes, John Earl; and Anderson, Kyrill M. *The Soviet World of American Communism*. New Haven, CT: Yale University Press, 1998.

Le Bon, Gustave. *The Psychology of Socialism*. New York: Macmillan, 1899.

Lee, Henry Garnsey. *Nothing But Praise*. Culver City, CA: Murray & Gee, 1948.

Lomborg, Bjorn. *The Skeptical Environmentalist: Measuring the Real State of the World*. New York: Cambridge University Press, 2001.

Maddison, Angus. *The World Economy: Historical Statistics*. Paris, France: Development Centre, Organisation for Economic Co-operation and Development, 2003.

Martin, Jerry L.; and Neal, Anne D. *Defending Civilization: How Our Universities are Failing America and What Can be Done About It*. American Council of Trustees and Alumni, 2002 • **http://www.goacta.org/ publications/Reports/defciv.pdf**

McPherson, James. *Battle Cry of Freedom*. New York: Oxford University Press, 2003.

Meadows, Donella; Meadows, Dennis; Randers, Jorgen; and Behrens III, William. *The Limits to Growth*. London: Potomac Associates, 1972.

Miles, Marc A.; Feulner, Jr., Edwin J.; and O'Grady, Mary Anastasia. *2004 Index of Economic Freedom*. Washington, D.C.: Heritage Foundation, 2004.

Moynahan, Brian. *The Russian Century*. New York: Random House, 1994.

National Bureau of Economic Research. *U.S. Business Cycle Expansion and Contractions*. Cambridge, MA: NBER, 2003.

National Review: **www.nationalreview.com**

Norberg, Johan. *In Defense of Global Capitalism*. Washington, D.C.: Cato Institute, 2003.

Nord, Mark; Andrews, Margaret; and Carlson, Steven. *Household Food Security in the United States, 2002*. U.S. Department of Agriculture, 2003.

Oswald, Andrew; and Zizzo, Daniel. "Are People Willing to Pay to Reduce Others' Incomes?" *Annales d'Economie et de Statistique*. July/December 2001: 63–64, 39–65.

Paige, Sean. "Shark Spin Soup." *National Review Online*, June 7, 2002.

Patterson, Orlando. *Slavery and Social Death: A Comparative Study*. Boston: Harvard University Press, 1985.

Rector, Robert E.; and Johnson, Kirk A. *Understanding Poverty in America.* Heritage Foundation Policy Report, Jan. 4, 2004.

Rhodes, Richard; and Beller, Denis. "The Need for Nuclear Power." *Foreign Affairs.* January/February 2000.

Robinson, John P.; and Godbey, Geoffrey. *Time for Life: the Surprising Ways Americans Use their Time.* University Park, PA: University of Pennsylvania Press, 1997.

Rogers, Jim. *Adventure Capitalist.* New York: Random House, 2003.

Satel, Sally. *PC, M.D.: How Political Correctness is Corrupting Medicine.* New York: Basic Books, 2002.

Schiller, Herbert I. *Communication and Cultural Domination.* Armonk, NY: E.M. Sharpe, 1976.

Shirer, William L. *The Rise and Fall of the Third Reich.* New York: Fawcett Crest, 1960.

Slesnick, Daniel. *Living Standards in the United States: A Consumption-Based Approach.* Washington, D.C.: AEI Press, 2000.

Stein, Herbert. *What I Think.* Washington, D.C.: AEI Press, 1998.

Sommers, Christina Hoff. *The War Against Boys: How Misguided Feminism is Harming Our Young Men.* New York: Simon & Schuster, 2001.

———. *Who Stole Feminism?* New York: Touchstone, 1994.

2004 Economic Report of the President. Baton Rouge, LA: Claitor's, 2004.

United Nations Department of Economic and Social Affairs, Population Division. *World Population Prospects: The 2002 Revision* • Website: **http://www.un.org/esa/population/unpop.htm**

United Nations Development Programme. *Human Development Report 1997* • **http://www.undp.org/dpa/publications/index.html**

United States Census Bureau. *Asset Ownership of Households: 1998 and 2000.*

———. *2003 Statistical Abstract of the United States.* Hoovers, Inc, 2004.

United States Department of Transportation, Federal Highway Administration. *Transportation Air Quality: Selected Facts and Figures.* 2001.

Victory at Sea. A&E Home Video, 2003 (rerelease of 1952 TV series).

Walsh, J.E.; Doran, P.T.; Priscu, J.C.; Lyons, W.B.; Fountain, A.G.; McKnight, D.M.; Moorhead, D.L.; Virginia, R.A.; Wall, D.H.; Chow, G.D.; Fritsen, C.H.; McKay, C.P.; and Parsons, A.N. "Climate Change (Communication Arising)—Recent Temperature Trends in the Antarctic." *Nature* 418(6895):292–292. 2002.

White, Matthew. *Historical Atlas of the Twentieth Century* • **http://users.erols.com/mwhite28/20centry.htm**

World Bank. *Global Economic Prospects 2003.* Washington, D.C.: World Bank, 2003.

World War II. New York: Primedia. Subscriptions: (800) 829-3340.

★★★ ★★★

ABOUT THE AUTHORS

Ben Stein is a graduate of Columbia University and Yale Law School. He has worked as a speechwriter for Presidents Nixon and Ford, a columnist and editorial writer for *The Wall Street Journal*, a law instructor at Pepperdine University, and a teacher of media studies at American University in Washington, D.C., and the University of California at Santa Cruz. He has written for *The American Spectator* for 30 years, and is a very frequent speaker. He is probably best known for his acting roles in *Ferris Bueller's Day Off* and *The Wonder Years* and for his long-running Emmy Award–winning game show, *Win Ben Stein's Money*. He is a regular television commentator and lives in Los Angeles with his wife and son. Website: **www.benstein.com**

Phil DeMuth was valedictorian of his class at the University of California, Santa Barbara, in 1972 (and was there when students in the adjacent town of Isla Vista burned down the Bank of America in 1970). He went on for his master's in communication and a Ph.D. in clinical psychology. He has written for *The Wall Street Journal* and *Barron's* as well as *Human Behavior* and *Psychology Today*. He is also co-author (with Ben Stein) of *Yes, You Can Time the Market!* and is an investment advisor in Los Angeles, California. Website: **www.phildemuth.com**

★★★ ★★★

NOTES

NOTES

NOTES

NOTES

NOTES

NOTES

NOTES

NOTES

NOTES

NOTES

NOTES

NOTES

✱ ✱ ✱

N B P

We hope you enjoyed this book. If you'd like to receive more information, please contact New Beginnings Press through their distributors:

Hay House, Inc.
P.O. Box 5100
Carlsbad, CA 92018-5100

(760) 431-7695 or **(800) 654-5126**
(760) 431-6948 (fax) or **(800) 650-5115 (fax)**
www.hayhouse.com

✱ ✱ ✱

Distributed in Australia by:
Hay House Australia Pty. Ltd. • 18/36 Ralph St. • Alexandria NSW 2015
Phone: 612-9669-4299 • *Fax:* 612-9669-4144 • www.hayhouse.com.au

Distributed in the United Kingdom by:
Hay House UK, Ltd. • Unit 62, Canalot Studios
222 Kensal Rd., London W10 5BN • *Phone:* 44-20-8962-1230
Fax: 44-20-8962-1239 • www.hayhouse.co.uk

Distributed in the Republic of South Africa by:
Hay House SA (Pty), Ltd., P.O. Box 990, Witkoppen 2068
Phone/Fax: 2711-7012233 • orders@psdprom.co.za

Distributed in Canada by:
Raincoast • 9050 Shaughnessy St., Vancouver, B.C. V6P 6E5
Phone: (604) 323-7100 • *Fax:* (604) 323-2600

✱ ✱ ✱